Social Media as Social Scie

Social media has put mass communication in the hands of normal people on an unprecedented scale, and has also given social scientists the tools necessary to listen to the voices of everyday people around the world. This book gives social scientists the skills necessary to leverage that opportunity and transform social media's vast stream of information into social science data. The book combines the big data techniques of computer science with social science methodology. Intended as a text for advanced undergraduates, graduate students, and researchers in the social sciences, this book provides a methodological pathway for scholars who want to make use of this new and evolving source of data. It provides a framework for building one's own data collection and analysis infrastructure, a toolkit of content analysis, geographic analysis, and network analysis, and meditations on the ethical implications of social media data.

Steven Lloyd Wilson is an assistant professor of politics at Brandeis University, project manager for the V-Dem Institute, and co-PI of the Digital Society Project. His research focuses on comparative democratization, cyber-security, and the effect of the Internet and social media on authoritarian regimes, particularly in the post-Soviet world.

Social Media as Social Science Data

Steven Lloyd Wilson

Brandeis University

CAMBRIDGE
UNIVERSITY PRESS

Shaftesbury Road, Cambridge CB2 8EA, United Kingdom

One Liberty Plaza, 20th Floor, New York, NY 10006, USA

477 Williamstown Road, Port Melbourne, VIC 3207, Australia

314–321, 3rd Floor, Plot 3, Splendor Forum, Jasola District Centre, New Delhi – 110025, India

103 Penang Road, #05–06/07, Visioncrest Commercial, Singapore 238467

Cambridge University Press is part of Cambridge University Press & Assessment, a department of the University of Cambridge.

We share the University's mission to contribute to society through the pursuit of education, learning and research at the highest international levels of excellence.

www.cambridge.org
Information on this title: www.cambridge.org/9781108496414

DOI: 10.1017/9781108677561

First published 2022

A catalogue record for this publication is available from the British Library.

ISBN 978-1-108-49641-4 Hardback
ISBN 978-1-108-73377-9 Paperback

Cambridge University Press & Assessment has no responsibility for the persistence or accuracy of URLs for external or third-party internet websites referred to in this publication and does not guarantee that any content on such websites is, or will remain, accurate or appropriate.

Contents

Figures

Tables

Code Snippets

Acknowledgments

This book had its start back in December of 2011, when the eruption of mass protest in Moscow coincided with the beginning of my winter break from Wisconsin's PhD program. I was supposed to be working on my comps and so naturally procrastinated by instead figuring out how to use Twitter's API to collect all of the tweets originating from Moscow in real time. Ten years and about ten billion archived tweets later, I've got a book to show for it. There are a lot of people to thank for how that circuitous path was traversed.

First, I would like to thank my dissertation chair, Yoi Herrera, who has been enormously supportive at every step. During grad school, she introduced me to any number of topics and methods that have found their way into nearly every page of this book. And since then, she has been a coauthor, mentor, and friend.

In addition, this project would never have come together into book form had John Gerring not asked on a call about a related project, "have you ever thought of writing a book about this?" I had not, but now I have. Thank you for that push, and for the extraordinary generosity of sharing your previous book proposals, and for being instrumental in connecting my proposal with its eventual publishing home.

Along the way, the manuscript has had the benefit of being presented piecemeal at too many panels, conferences, and workshops to count. But of special note are the 2018 and 2019 authors' workshops at Syracuse that gave incredibly rich and constructive feedback as the book developed into its present form. And, in particular, Colin Elman's guidance through the publication process and patience with a first-time author's utter underestimation of the time it would take to write a book are deeply appreciated. And Colin is also to thank for recommending that I include a chapter on the ethics of social media data, along with a starting set of citations, for a chapter that I now can't imagine the book without.

I also owe deep gratitude to the innumerable students and coauthors along the way who constantly pushed me to learn and develop new ways to collect and use social media data both for use in their research and for projects we've coauthored. The toolkit I present in this book is the product of long years of always trying to say yes to anyone who could think of a use for data I'd collected, or could think of new data they needed that I didn't yet know how to collect.

Massive data projects like this cannot exist without dedicated IT staff and computing departments at the various institutions I've called home. While for the first few years my social media data collection occurred on an old video game computer in my home office, along the way and as it grew the collection has been graciously housed and supported in turn by the V-Dem Institute at the University of Gothenburg, the University of Nevada, Reno, NYU's Center for Social Media and Politics (CSMaP), and Brandeis University.

I can never thank my mom and dad enough, for a lifetime of support and confidence, and for always being interested in the research I do. My love of learning and science began with a childhood of library used-book sales and a loving home in which to read them all. I wish my grandparents could have seen this, but when I still could, I delighted in explaining to them the beginnings of this project all those years ago.

My Annie, my partner in all this, has been my rock for everything. There isn't a word or concept in all of this that she hasn't patiently listened to me explain a dozen times over, and she has endured the years of work and celebrated with me in the moments of joy. And last, but never least, my pack of incorrigibles, Amber and Ashlee and Taffy and Lilo and Whiskers and Amanda and Weezer and Merry, have made every day worth the while.

1   Why Social Media Matters to the Social Sciences

In 1989, millions of protesters filled the streets of China, with some estimates putting the peak number in the hundreds of millions, though it is unlikely that true statistics will ever be known. Our minute-by-minute knowledge of those last days, and of the massacre in Tiananmen Square at their climax, is patchy at best. And what little understanding we do have is due largely to the battalion of foreign journalists who happened to be in Beijing at that exact time to cover a Sino-Soviet summit.

Thirty years later, such a paucity of preserved information is unimaginable outside of a handful of increasingly isolated cases, as protests in the most authoritarian of states are accompanied by a cavalcade of tweets, blogs, social media posts, and amateur photography. The Arab Spring and Color Revolutions highlighted this phenomenon: events tracked to the minute, electronic coordination of opposition action, publication of atrocity in real time, the names and faces of both martyrs and villains universally publicized. The Internet seems toxic to the old authoritarian standbys of social atomization and persistent secrecy.

Consider the famous photographs associated with Tiananmen Square and those from Tahrir Square. The former are grainy, taken from a vast distance at a high angle. The famous "tank man" in the iconic photograph is grabbed and escorted away moments later – whether by desperate friends or state security we have never conclusively learned – and his identity remains unknown to this day. One of the most iconic photographs in history features a man whose name we do not know, and only exists in the historical record at all because of the chance presence of foreign journalists. The world didn't see these pictures for quite some time, as they were shot through telescopic lenses peeking through closed curtains, the film hurriedly hidden inside toilet tanks minutes before the arrival of state security, and then smuggled out of the country days later.

Contrast that with the images taken in Tahrir Square during the mass uprising in Egypt amid the Arab Spring. Those photos are high resolution, perfectly crisp, and taken at street level. The photos were posted online within moments of being taken, and circulated around the world on millions of screens small and large. The famous image of a protester standing alone with upraised sign before the might of the state is in this case not an unknown revolutionary, but in fact was instantly identified. You could follow him on Twitter and read his blog within moments of seeing him flicker across your screen.

More information is published by more people today than at any time in human history. The era of mass consumption of media has given way to an era of mass production. Numbers confound easy comprehension, and give way to colorful illustration: The amount of text posted to Twitter every day is the equivalent of some 8 000 copies of *War and Peace*, more photos are uploaded to Facebook every day than exist in all of human history prior to 1990. It's not that thousands of great novels are being written every day, but that a source of human communication is now being recorded, where before it was lost to historical entropy. Internet communications, recorded in an infinite proliferation of magnetic bits, are enshrining the low background noise of human society: the diaries, snippets of conversation, personal letters, and oral histories that once faded from records, but are now archived away digitally.

This is the key challenge of social media as "big data": it is not just that it represents *more* data than we have ever had to deal with before, but that it represents *different* data than we have had access to. Quantity, as Stalin might have said, is a quality all its own.

1.1 The Theory of Why It Matters

Two schools of thought have developed around the effect of the Internet and social media upon society. Some insist that the effect these technologies have is but incremental, building on print, telephones, radio, and television. Others argue that the information revolution is truly a *revolution*, a seismic shift in the balance of power between peoples and states comparable only to the fruition of Gutenberg in the nineteenth century. The reality, as many scholars have argued over the last decade, rests somewhere between the two extremes.

A slightly tangential body of work provides perhaps the best model for understanding why social media is important to us as social scientists: the literature of how mass literacy transformed society in the nineteenth century. Gellner (and to a lesser degree Anderson) argued that states needed to encourage mass literacy (and the social changes it wrought) in order to industrialize, but then reaped the consequences of increased public capacities for collective action that culminated in nationalism (Anderson, 1983; Gellner, 1983). Gellner notes that mass literacy fundamentally changed the structure of society during the course of modernization. Preliterate societies were highly stratified, the population of each strata non-interchangeable with others. State-sponsored education flattened the postliterate societal structure, churning out masses of technically equal citizens, interchangeable parts in the machinery of industry. The political and social implications of this change were profound, giving birth to the age of mass movements. The economic motivation of elites in sponsoring mass literacy had the unintended consequence of the whirlwind of mass consciousness.

In the modern setting, we see a parallel paradox. Power-holding elites exist in a tension between wanting to open up communication (in order to assess public support, efficiently set placating policy, and reap the benefits of globalized trade that depends on these new communications technologies) while simultaneously wanting to repress communication in order to prevent the organization of opposition. The pressure of the International Telecommunications Union during the 1990s to open up telecoms industries globally was premised on promises of the economic benefits that it would bring regimes otherwise disinclined toward openness or liberalization. And similar to mass literacy's unintended consequences, the opening of telecommunications laid the groundwork for worldwide internet access. While it is hopelessly utopian to suggest that the Internet is uncensorable or a magic guaranteer of free speech in the face of authoritarianism, it has undeniably altered the capacity of populations to communicate. Communication, the flow of information, is the heart blood of society. It is what determines how and why our societies organize, who ends up with power, what our social structure looks like. And so something that drastically changes the way communication works, inevitably alters society itself.

In preliterate societies, information could cheaply flow within a particular social stratum, but crossing strata was more expensive. This had two effects. First, social movements in preliterate societies tended to be intrastrata. Second, the flow of information between ruler and ruled was more limited than that within strata. The natural governmental equilibrium during this period would be despotic, because the poor flow of information between strata would make interstrata collective action less likely. The strongest individual stratum could maintain control by force over the other strata, and because of the high cost of interstrata collective action, a noncoercive equilibrium was unlikely.

By collapsing the boundaries between strata, the advent of mass literacy altered the flow of information in society. Social movements could draw from the bulk of the population, leading variously to democratic or authoritarian outcomes. The key feature of this era was that while receiving information became universal and cheap, the transmission of information, while cheaper than previously, was still proportionately much more expensive than receiving. This era is characterized by universal reception of information, but with the transmission of information centralized in a small number of power holders. While social movements could become more massive, they also became less precise. In Tilly's many works on contentious politics and social movements throughout history, he identifies in particular the way that repertoires of social action evolved with the changing nature of the state during this period (Tilly, 2002, 2003).

The spread of the Internet and new communications technologies changes the flow of information again, and in doing so changes the resulting solutions to collective action problems. While receiving information gets even cheaper with widespread internet access, transmitting information also becomes cheap. In a general sense, the effect of modern communications is to effectively eliminate the transaction costs of both receiving and sending information.

To derive an understanding of how the Internet changes society, it is first necessary to think through how exactly the Internet differs from previous iterations of communications technologies. One way to compare different communications technologies is by comparing the relative costs to send and receive information, and how that cost scales to larger numbers of individuals with each technology. Figure 1.1 displays the number of people being reached by

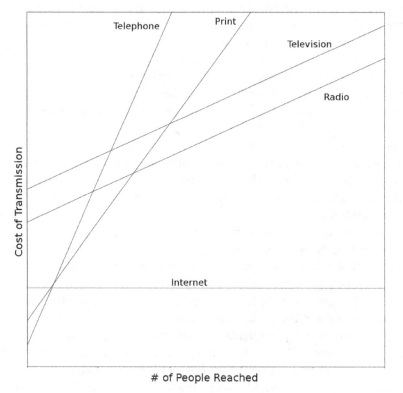

Figure 1.1 Cost of transmission as a function of number of recipients

a particular transmission on the x-axis, and the cost required to do so by the transmitting individual on the y-axis. The cost curves of each technology demonstrate both the fixed-cost barriers of entry into particular types of transmission (represented by the y-intercepts of each curve) and the marginal cost associated with using that transmission technology (the slopes of the curves). I have plotted theoretical cost curves for several important communications technologies. Television, requiring the enormous fixed cost of transmitters, has the highest fixed cost and its curve increases monotonically but relatively slowly. Radio, a very similar technology to television, has a similar curve, but shifted to a lower cost.

Telephone and print are instructive cases, in that the former involves extremely low fixed costs for the end user, but scales very badly due to its essentially one-to-one design. Print media begins with a higher fixed cost than telephony, and scales better, but does not scale as well as television and radio for very large numbers of recipients. The novelty of the Internet is that while traditional computers entail a moderate fixed cost (moderate in comparison to building a television transmitter, that is), they scale almost infinitely well with a marginal cost of nearly zero to reach more and more individuals with each transmission. As the cost of computers decreases, that horizontal curve shifts downward. The value of smartphones in this context is that they graft the minimal fixed costs of telephony to the minuscule marginal costs of transmission associated with computers.

This perfect scaling effect is what makes internet communications distinct from every previous communications technology, and is the theoretical basis for why social media emerged in the contemporary world. Social media represents infinitely scaling, low fixed-cost communication taken to its logical extreme. Every person on the planet able to communicate with no effort or expense with every other person on the planet.

1.2 Using Social Media Data

Early social media research focused on studying what exactly it was, and how it affected existing variables of interest. That is, this is literature in which social media is the dependent or independent variable. The greatest body of this early literature focused on the connection between social media and mass mobilization, in both authoritarian and democratic contexts (Farrell, 2012; Howard et al., 2011; Tufekci and Wilson, 2012; Wilson, 2017). In addition to the extensive article-length works, mobilization and social media have been explored in standout books from Clay Shirky (*Here Comes Everybody*) and

Manuel Castells (*Networks of Outrage and Hope*) (Castells, 2015; Shirky, 2009). The use of the Internet and social media in general in politics and society has been well covered by Cristian Vaccari's *Digital Politics in Western Democracies*, Christian Fuchs' *Social Media: A Critical Introduction*, Persily and Tucker's *Social Media and Democracy*, and Internet and Politics handbooks from both Routledge and Oxford (Chadwick and Howard, 2010; Dutton, 2013; Fuchs, 2017; Persily and Tucker, 2020; Vaccari, 2013). While constantly maturing, the study of social media as a phenomenon has evolved alongside the technology itself. For example, disinformation (and misinformation) campaigns via bots and trolls on social media have intensified, and have been made especially salient by their prominence in the last few American electoral cycles (Starbird, 2019).

The second wave of social media research emerged focusing on the use of it as data for the measurement of offline phenomena. It treats social media usage and content not as an independent or dependent variable itself, but as a new method for measurement alongside surveys, interviews, and other tried and true methods. This second genre of literature is still in its infancy relative to these established methods, with projects targeting a plethora of different research goals across the social sciences. These include applications as varied as Carlos Castillo's book *Big Crisis Data* using social media to detect when and where natural disasters occur (Castillo, 2016), comparison of traditional media content versus social media content during natural disasters (Vieweg et al., 2010), the study of information diffusion through a networked population (Jansen et al., 2009; Lerman and Ghosh, 2010; Romero et al., 2011), the prediction of shifts in the stock market based on tweet analysis (Bollen, Mao, and Zeng, 2011; Si et al., 2013), and how social media affects informal communication in the workplace (Zhao and Rosson, 2009).

In addition, a number of long-term and collaborative research projects are working on using social media as general measurement tools. In this arena, one standout is the Center for Social Media and Politics (CSMaP) at New York University led by Bonneau, Nagler, and Tucker, which has produced dozens of publications, datasets, policy white papers, and research tools. This scholarship runs the gamut from misinformation on social media (Guess, Nagler, and Tucker, 2019; Munger et al., 2022; Sanderson et al., 2021; Tucker et al., 2018), to political mobilization and protest on social media (Jost et al., 2018; Metzger and Tucker, 2017; Munger et al., 2019), to extensive software tools in both Python and R made available for free to the scientific community (CSMaP, 2022; Padmakumar and Terechshenko, 2020).

Additional significant institutional collaborations include the Social Media Lab (SoMe Lab) at the University of Washington. Led by Mason, Spiro, and Starbird, the lab has published exceptional scholarship, especially in the usage of network analysis techniques across social media datasets (Reed, Spiro, and Butts, 2016; Wilson and Starbird, 2020). And at Northeastern, David Lazer's lab has published widely as well with dozens of academic articles and the seminal big-picture piece of scholarship *Meaningful Measures of Human Society in the Twenty-First Century* (Lazer et al., 2021).

Finally, the cross-university effort of the Digital Society Project has focused on large-n cross-country measurements of a variety of aspects of social media, including the ability of governments to censor and monitor social media, the prevalence of misinformation on the social media of each country, and the usage of social media to mobilize offline action of various sorts (Mechkova et al., 2019; Wilson, Lindberg, and Tronvoll, 2021; Wilson and Wiysonge, 2020).

Despite the exciting opportunities afforded by this new form of data, its usage involves a number of methodological challenges, both in terms of collection and measurement. Ruths and Pfeffer's article "Social Media for Large Studies of Behavior" in *Science* outlined the major obstacles to using social media as a direct source of data (Ruths and Pfeffer, 2014). Zachary Steinert-Threlkeld's *Twitter as Data* provides an excellent primer for the methods needed to get started collecting and analyzing tweets (Steinert-Threlkeld, 2018).

While scholars have made individual advances in resolving methodological challenges for their own particular projects, there has yet to be a general text that pulls together the methodologies of social media research into a cohesive framework. And problematically, many of the techniques for collecting social media data have remained locked behind programming technical expertise not particularly common in the social sciences. As such, this book provides an "on-ramp" for social scientists who want to use social media data in their research, regardless of what level of computer science expertise they currently possess. This book functions as a guide for scholars to thinking about the methodological problems inherent in social media data, and how to rigorously compensate for those problems such that the data can be held to the same scientific standards as surveys and other similar data.

This book is intended as a text for advanced undergraduates, graduate students, and researchers in the social sciences. Four broad uses of it as a text are envisioned. First, it serves as the primary textbook for courses explicitly focused on the usage of social media in the social sciences (such as Internet and Politics courses). Second, it provides a methodological supplement for substantive courses in Comparative and American Politics, allowing students to personally collect and utilize real data for their research topics using this new source of data. Throughout the book, example applications are pulled from a variety of global contexts, from the populations of the developing world to the social media activity of elites in the American government. Third, it functions as an applied toolkit to be plugged into research methods courses. Fourth, it offers a reference for researchers who want to utilize social media data in their research, but currently lack the technical ability to get started on their own.

Chapter 2 introduces the building blocks of an infrastructure for collecting social media data. It includes a summary of what data is available via Twitter, and how we can best structure a collection system in general for any number of social science applications. In addition, it walks through how to collect a worldwide sample of all posted tweets in real time, along with database and compression tools for ensuring that the infrastructure can be used for long-term data collection projects encompassing millions of data points.

The next three chapters provide detailed discussion of three of the major methods used for analyzing social media data. Chapter 3 focuses on content analysis and introduces the collection of data from Twitter by either select keywords or languages. It then develops computerized content analysis techniques for use on tweets, covering the particular challenges of adapting these techniques for usage on the text from social media (for instance, dealing with the often very short passages of text, the especially dense usage of colloquialisms, and the frequent mixing of different languages within a particular source of social media text data). It also covers the download of other forms of content (such as video and images) and the handling of meta-objects such as mentions and hashtags.

One of the most exciting types of social media data are geolocated data, which include the source location of the post, based on the GPS capabilities of the posting device. Chapter 4 discusses the particular advantages offered by this data, including the capacity to perform extremely fine-grained subnational studies impossible with traditional sources of data. In addition, the chapter provides software for processing geocoded social media data in order to efficiently identify the country and subnational unit of every tweet in a collection, including an example application collecting *all* geocoded tweets in the world.

Chapter 5 introduces network analysis. Social media data frequently has elements that are amenable to network analysis, including friend/follower networks and retweet networks. This chapter addresses how to collect and operationalize this data into measures appropriate for network analysis. It shows how to collect en masse the timelines of a given set of users, in addition to traversing their friend and follower networks. In addition, it demonstrates how to do so by collecting all tweets of all members of Congress in real time. Finally, it demonstrates in applied form how to identify automated accounts (bots) among the data being collected.

Finally, the book concludes with Chapter 6's discussion of the particular ethical concerns raised by using social media data. This includes data privacy concerns, for instance the need in some contexts to anonymize unique user identifiers in all stored tweets so that not even the researchers have access to user names and such. In addition, the chapter reviews concerns frequently raised by institutional review boards in terms of human subjects research, and some of the thorny issues raised by the terms of use of social media sites with regard to data sharing and replicability. In particular, it will walk through what scholars need to know about the limitations imposed by Twitter's terms of use, what use cases are considered acceptable use (sharing data among researchers on the same project), and strategies for common scholarly needs that fall within gray areas (e.g. providing word frequency matrices so that content analysis can be fully replicated, but the terms of use conditions regarding republication of tweets are not violated).

Throughout, the book includes sample data and fully functional Python code in order to allow readers to proceed with their own collection and analysis of social media data. In particular, all source code is explained in full, and made fully available via the book's GitHub repository. Most importantly, all of the code in this book is built for use on real data, often in large quantities. Applications that work on small artificial datasets tend to break down and not scale when confronted with real data projects involving big data. As such, this book avoids using "toy" data and applications as examples throughout in order to ensure that the techniques are always explained in the context of real applications for real research.

By necessity of brevity, it focuses on using Twitter as the social media platform of choice simply because the public application programming interface and widespread support of the platform makes it the easiest to connect to and use for the broadest range of social science projects. However, the infrastructure constructed throughout the book, and the concepts and methods developed, are universal in the sense that they can be adapted and repurposed for any particular social media site.

Social media has put mass communication in the hands of normal people on an unprecedented scale, and has also given social scientists the tools necessary to *listen* to the everyday speech of everyday people around the world. This books aims to give social scientists the skills necessary to leverage that opportunity, and transform social media's infinite stream of information into social science data.

2 Getting Started with Social Media Data

What is social media data? There is a huge variety of social media platforms out there, with all sorts of different types of content and focuses of their functionality. YouTube centers itself on sharing videos. TikTok integrates short-form user videos with algorithms linking on the basis of content rather than user linkages. Various blogging platforms host more long-form text. Reddit resembles old bulletin board software with content framed around threaded discussion, and its upvoting system powerfully decentralizes what content is seen, decoupled from the algorithms that characterize other sites. Facebook has a mix of types of content, while focusing heavily on the social networking, and increasingly as a portal for providing a walled garden of content driven by algorithm. Twitter is perhaps the simplest: just short snippets of text listed traditionally in order of posting and with virtually everything public by default.

Twitter is a particularly interesting source of data, since so much of its content is posted from mobile devices, meaning that its textual content is generated as events occur by individuals on the ground, as opposed to after the fact. This makes the content published on Twitter a sort of communication that has only been rarely recorded in previous history, and never at this scale. It is also by far the most commonly used source of social media data by researchers.

That popularity among researchers is primarily because of two reasons. First, Twitter is global in reach, which means that data is available from virtually every country on the planet. It is far from the largest social media platform: its number of active users is dwarfed by Facebook, for instance. And there is of course a monumental level of variance between different countries, and significant exceptions like China exist in which Twitter is banned almost entirely. However, compared to any other microblogging platform, and compared to the industry leader in each of the other categories of social media platforms, Twitter is the closest thing we have to universal in reach. Second, Twitter itself has provided extensive support for researchers to search their archives and collect data from their backend databases. This has democratized research, with a terrifically low barrier of entry to collect Twitter data such that anyone with an internet connection and a little bit of technical savvy can collect enough textual data to fill libraries if printed out.

In this chapter, I will first walk through what data is available from Twitter, discuss various caveats and some historical context for how certain elements evolved, and then provide detailed walkthroughs both of what the raw data looks like, and how to actually collect and process it. By the end of this chapter, you will be able to set up a basic infrastructure for downloading and analyzing tweets en masse.

2.1 What Is Twitter Data?

Twitter's functionality is one of emergent complexity, built on a minimalist concept. Users post brief messages (tweets) that are displayed publicly. An individual user's page on Twitter is effectively a log of their activity: simply a list of the messages they have posted displayed in reverse chronological order. Each user can follow other users, which creates the concept of the "feed," which is simply showing a user the messages of anyone they follow, again traditionally in simple reverse chronological order.

Many of the additional functions we associate with Twitter are merely tweaks of this basic formula. Retweets are essentially just a user taking someone else's tweet and reposting it under their name. Comments on tweets are just additional tweets linked to the previous one. Images, audio, and video are just URLs typed into the body of the tweet and then interpreted and rendered by the web browser.

Hashtags are words with the "#" symbol prepended (such as "#GoBadgers") that signal that the word in question has to do with that topic, which can then be searched for by others. This allows users to self-index what they are posting and be part of a larger discussion without the need for additional layers of complexity like an interface for prompting users to enter keywords.

Tweeting "at" someone simply means including their username, prepended by an "@" symbol. This is called a "mention" and any time someone is mentioned they are notified. So it is a way of including someone else in a conversation.

But what unifies all of these small features is that they are merely prede-termined ways of interpreting the text of the tweet itself. There is no separate database structure indicating which users are mentioned in a particular tweet, no attachments stored somewhere as with emails when an image or video is included, no one-to-many relational database linking individual tweets to which topics that tweet is associated with. Twitter is incredibly simple underneath the hood: Every tweet is just a short chunk of text that has a plethora of emergent properties based on simple user-created marking-up of that text.

This makes collecting and processing Twitter data deceptively simple because for all the enormous size of such databases, and a variety of complexity we might add due to our research interests in particular words, hashtags, user relationships, or network models of communication, the data itself always can be distilled back to short blocks of text that we extract all of that other information from.

And that text is short, putting the "micro" in the term microblogs. Historically, tweets were limited to 140 characters of text, because that was also the length limit of SMS (i.e. text) messages. That length limit was in turn determined by the fact that it corresponded to the amount of ASCII encoded text that could fit into a single packet of information on cell phone networks. Text messaging was not a feature designed into cellular networks, but something hacked onto it after the fact by clever programmers. Even when not actively being used, an individual cell phone constantly pings the network with empty packets in order to check to see if there is an incoming call. If there is no call, the network pings back with another empty packet in order to indicate that yes, you have successfully connected, but no, there is nothing to do right now. It occurred to some engineers that they could stuff a tiny amount of text into that otherwise empty packet, and thus text messages were invented. The nature of tweets was thus intertwined from their inception with cell phone networks, and so the eventual rise of smartphones and the integration of their GPS capabilities with Twitter should be seen as a natural evolution.

2.2 Accessing Twitter Data

There are three ways to collect Twitter data, underneath all of the packages and interfaces that help you out: the streaming API, the search API, and through third-party databases. Even if you never write barebones code to access the Twitter API, it is important to know the distinctions between the different techniques, and the limitations of the interface, in order to understand the limitations on your ability to collect data.

An API is an "application programming interface," which just means a set of tools to allow you to write computer code to access someone else's application. That is, in order to access tweets, one does not typically sit down and write a web scraper and point it at Twitter. Instead, we use the API provided by Twitter that provides much more powerful tools that hook into their backend databases. So instead of writing hundreds of lines of custom web-scraping code, Twitter has helpfully already written code to do most of the heavy lifting.

The Twitter API is the main reason why Twitter is by far the most common source of social media data used in academic research. Its ease of use, and capacity for downloading truly staggering amounts of data, makes it a very attractive tool for researchers. The lowering of the threshold of entry for this data source has been a boon for social scientists, as it has democratized access to data so that virtually no funding or resources are necessary for academics to do so. But this is also a double-edged sword, as the easy access has led to a proliferation of sloppy science in which the issues discussed in this chapter become deeply problematic.

In particular, Twitter introduced a new Academic API in the spring of 2021, which has increased the capacity of researchers to access large quantities of data (capped at a limit of 10 million tweet downloads per month). This tier of access allows access to both the 1.1 API endpoints and the new 2.0 ones. Elevation of one's developer account on Twitter to the academic tier is free, but does require submitting an application detailing what sort of research you will be using the API for, and verifying that you are a grad student, academic researcher, or professor. The code in this book requires access to the 1.1 endpoints as they are the longest in service, most stable, and still offer the most comprehensive data compared to the 2.0 endpoints.

2.2.1 The Search API

The search API is by far the simplest way of accessing tweets en masse, but is also the most limited in terms of quantity, scope, and usability. This access point requires only a Twitter account to access and allows searches to be run returning tweets in the standard JSON (JavaScript Object Notation) format. Searches can be based on either geographic area (specifying nearness to a defined place name) or through latitude-longitude boxes.

There are two major limitations. First, by default the search API only searches the last seven days of tweets, making it unsuitable for digging into any topic that is not strictly contemporaneous. In addition, it means that researchers have been forced to rely on lucking into data being available after the fact, or upon making the decision to archive data as an event of interest begins to happen. The former is obviously unreliable, but the latter is a dangerous and systemic selection upon the dependent variable, because comparable data from when interesting events are not happening, is not being archived for comparative purposes.

Second, the search is not comprehensive, returning an ill-defined subset of the tweets that actually match the search terms. Twitter has not been particularly transparent about the process by which this subset is arrived at. Researchers have undertaken projects to describe the differences in tweets that are returned from different sources (Alkulaib et al., 2019; Campan et al., 2018; Chen, Duan, and Yang, 2021; Morstatter, Pfeffer, and Liu, 2014). To do so they used the search API to search for a set of predetermined terms after the fact, the streaming API to collect tweets matching those terms in real time, and paid a company with firehose access for the tweets they had that matched those words.[1] In theory, all three sources should return the exact same set of tweets, however this was not the case. That work showed that the search and streaming APIs both tended to return fewer retweets than actually existed in the full firehose stream. It is hypothesized that this is due to Twitter wanting to prioritize finding distinctly different content when searches are performed.

The new academic API has made the use of search far more attractive for researchers, as it allows arbitrary searching over any time period, with a limit of 10 million tweet downloads per month. This allows academic researchers to get around the seven-day search limit, even if it means some limitations in terms of overall number of tweets that can be downloaded over a period of time. This text assumes that readers are using the academic API, which offers access to both the old 1.1 endpoints and the new 2.0 API endpoints.

2.2.2 The Streaming API

The streaming API is more complicated to set up and maintain, but has advantages that make it worth it. The primary distinction of the streaming API is that whatever search is performed, results are returned in real time, rather than as a lump quantity of previous tweets. This requires a more complicated software setup because rather than just manually running one-off searches, a researcher needs to set up a continuously running bit of software that is always running and dealing with new data as it comes in. In addition, accessing the streaming API requires registering a developer account with Twitter and passing along the unique alphanumeric dentifiers Twitter assigns to your project, rather than just using a simple login and password associated with a normal account on Twitter's website.

It is critical to realize the core limitation of the streaming API: Once you set up a search, you will only receive results from then on. This means that the streaming API is worthless for trying to search for content after the fact. A scholar needs to already be searching for whatever it is that interests them before the fact. This can be deeply problematic when items of interest are only identified after they occur. For instance, if a researcher realized that the Euromaidan protests in Ukraine might be valuable to their research after the protests started, they would not be able to use the streaming API to access those tweets using the hashtag of "#euromaidan" once they realized it was important.

---

[1] The "firehose" is the term Twitter uses for the full real-time stream of *all* tweets, so called because trying to consume it is like trying to drink from a firehose.

On the other hand, the streaming API has the advantage of being immune to modification of tweets after the fact. Since the tweets are being downloaded in real time as they are posted, later deletion by either the user or Twitter will not affect your archive. This can be particularly important if doing research on topics that are politically sensitive enough that we might expect ex post facto self-censorship or deletions by Twitter itself to be common and systematic.

For instance, any researcher interested in the use of social media by terrorist groups such as the Islamic State will face insurmountable and systematic data missingness problems if the tweets are only searched for after the fact due to Twitter's campaign to systematically remove such accounts. While new accounts pop up as fast as the old are taken down in a perverse game of terrorist whack-a-mole, the fact that the old tweets are constantly being deleted from the archives means searching the archives misses a huge component of the content actually available from moment to moment on Twitter. Similar situations prevail in the case of many bodies of tweets of substantive interest: hate groups, alt-right groups, and of course the now legendary astroturfing campaigns of secessionist and Black Lives Matter groups invented by Russian operators during the 2016 American elections.

In addition, users of Twitter are familiar with the phenomenon of taking screenshots of particularly offensive tweets (especially from public figures like politicians) in order to "keep the receipts" should the individual inevitably backtrack and delete the offending tweet. The ability of users to sanitize their history of tweets is a critical problem with using any of the nonstreaming access points into Twitter's archives, and a strong point in favor of using the streaming API.

2.2.3 Other Access

There are technically other ways of accessing Twitter data, though they tend to be unsuitable for individual academic researchers due to cost and thus fall outside the intended scope of this book. First, it is possible to simply pay for any number of tweets from third-party companies. For context, the full real-time stream of all tweets worldwide is called the "firehose" by Twitter and is accessible only to a handful of large corporate clients. Those clients pay Twitter exorbitantly for that access and their business model is in collecting all tweets and selling batches of them to clients, based on either searches or internal analytics. For academic researchers, it is likely that the academic API will render the usage of expensive third-party sources moot, but if the quantity of tweets needed significantly exceeds the 10 million tweets per month cap, this can still be useful for researchers with sufficient research funds.

In addition, Twitter has donated the full archive of tweets to the Library of Congress for posterity. This gargantuan database of some hundred trillion individual tweets is currently completely inaccessible to researchers, and as of yet there are no publicly revealed plans for how the data will be curated and made accessible to the public or to scholars. The archive seems to be in a frustrating limbo, in which even if researchers produce their own funds and a plan for using the archive, there is no means for providing that access. As such, scholars should be prepared to collect their own data directly, or from one of the companies that provide access to their own curated archives.

2.3 The Nuts and Bolts of the Data

While the data available from tweets seems relatively straightforward at face value, there are a number of caveats that researchers should know about. This is due to both unexpected inconsistencies in the actual data, and confusing details about the structure of the data largely due to pressure for historical compatibility. While there is a plethora of metadata included with each downloaded tweet we will focus on several key ones in this book: the text of the tweet, the latitude and longitude from which the tweet was sent (if available), which user posted the tweet, along with metadata about the user including their time zone, language, number of friends, and number of followers. Snippet 2.1 shows the raw form of a very simple tweet pulled from the Twitter API. Actual downloaded tweets will contain many more fields and a lot of redundant data in various places, but this distilled version shows most of the key features.[2]

Note that the tweet data is all in plain text, so it's easy to write your own code to deal with it, or to just glance at the raw output to make sure your application is working fine. The structure is a format called JSON, which basically means that the structure is self-defining. That is, there are labels for all the data built right into the data so that it's human readable. Curly braces (i.e. { and }) wrap around nested objects, and individual items have a label followed by a colon and then the corresponding data. Commas separate data items, and square brackets (i.e. [and]) specify that inside is an array (i.e. an unlabeled list).

---

[2] Throughout this book, we connect to the v1.1 endpoints of the Twitter API, which are available for access via the academic API. The v2.0 endpoints differ and provide a very different JSON output, that is customized per request. Because there is more comprehensive data available via the 1.1 endpoints, I recommend using those except in cases where functionality is only provided via the 2.0 endpoints.

```
1  {
2    "created_at": "Thu May 10 17:41:57 +0000 2018",
3    "id": 994633657141813248,
4    "text": "The text of a tweet to @NASA informing them
5        Watney lives. #martian #spacepirates",
6    "lang": "en",
7    "user": {
8        "id": 944480690,
9        "screen_name": "groundcontrol",
10       "followers_count": 301211,
11       "friends_count": 101,
12       "statuses_count": 1010,
13       "time_zone": "PST",
14       "lang": "ru"
15   },
16   "coordinates": {
17       "coordinates": [-75.14310264,40.05701649]
18   },
19   "entities": {
20       "hashtags": [...],
21       "urls": [...],
22       "user_mentions": [...],
23       "media": [...]
24   }
25 }
26
```

Code Snippet 2.1 Example of tweet JSON object

While these fields may seem relatively self-explanatory, there are a number of complications and complexities that researchers should be aware of. We will now walk through these fields, slightly out of order so that they can be grouped in ways that make sense.

2.3.1 Unique Ids

The "id" field on line 3 is a very large integer that uniquely identifies the tweet. This allows you to find the tweet again after the fact on Twitter, and also is helpful for data management purposes to uniquely identify each tweet in your own database. On line 8, the "id" field inside the "user" object is in turn the unique identifier of the user who posted the tweet. This is useful for either looking up the details of the user after the fact (even if their screen name changes) and for keeping a database of your own for user tracking. In addition, this user identifier is used in a number of other fields not listed in this example in order to do things like reference when one tweet is in reply to another user's tweet.

Note however that these integers are *very* large, larger than the default maximum integer for most software. This is a natural side effect of just how many tweets have been posted, and how many user accounts exist, but it's important to keep in mind because it means special precautions need to be taken when dealing with that field in software. Excel, for example, will turn the last few digits of these ids into zeros, unless on import you tell it to treat it as a text field instead of a numerical field. R by default cannot handle numbers this large either and so it's necessary to install a package like bit64 in order to preserve that field. It is also larger than the maximum "integer" in most database software and so the field type in those cases needs to be set to "big integer" or the appropriate equivalent. If you run into difficulties with handling numbers this large in your software, it's always an option to simply tell the software to treat it as text instead as no applications on the user side will actually use it as a number (i.e. performing arithmetic).

2.3.2 User Data

The "user" object that begins on line 7 contains a number of fields within it that are of use. This is just a selection of some of the most useful fields, but the full API contains much more data about each user. In this example, the user's "screen_name" is listed right after the "id." This is the publicly visible name that the user goes by on Twitter, and if you go to someone's Twitter page is what you will see in the URL of the page. In addition there are three different counts (lines 10, 11, and 12) that represent metadata that can be important for certain applications. Followers count is the number of followers the user has, friends count is the number of users that they in turn follow, and statuses count is the number of statuses they have ever posted. The first two are very useful for network analysis purposes (which will be discussed at length in Chapter 5), while the last one gives an idea of how frequently the user posts. The important caveat for each of these is that the data returned is current as of the moment of the tweet being posted. That is, the follower count corresponds to how many followers the user had at the moment they posted this tweet, not as of the moment when the researcher searches for and downloads this tweet. As such, these fields are very useful in a streaming context of data collection, but if scraping tweets en masse after the fact, they will all return the same value for a certain user for every tweet.

2.3.3 The Tweet Text Itself

While the "text" field spanning lines 4 and 5 of our example seems to be straightforwardly reporting the text of the tweet, it is not quite that simple due to historical complications with keeping the API consistent. On a limited basis at the start of 2017, Twitter began allowing longer tweets, with a cap of 280 characters instead. This limit does not have a technical basis like the original 140-character one did, and so for purposes of long-term compatibility, one should probably keep in mind that the 280-character limit could easily be changed again now that the precedent for doing so has been set. By the end of 2017, the cap was raised to 280 characters for all users on Twitter.

This history is relevant because it has implications for the data being collected, especially if any historical data is included. The "text" field in a downloaded tweet does not include the full text of a 280-character tweet as one might expect, but instead is truncated to 140-characters. The reason for this is that the 140-character limit was in place for so long and was so fundamental to the platform that a decade of third-party code accessing the API had been written assuming that field would contain at most 140 characters of text. So when the cap was lifted, Twitter opted to play it very safe in terms of not breaking the compatibility of code that had made that assumption.

As such, Twitter added a new field called "full_text" that includes the full text of the tweet. However, since this field did not exist in the API prior to the raising of the cap, writing code to simply access this field will break if you also have tweets from prior to the raising of the cap. This means that if you are getting tweets from before and after that point, you may need to write code to accommodate it and pull from the appropriate field depending on the age of the tweet. In addition, if a user replies to or retweets another tweet, there will be an object that contains the full data (including text) of the original tweet as well. This can be important when dealing with retweets, since often retweets are posted with no original text from the user, so all that is displayed is the quoted text. We will deal more with the complexities like this as appropriate in Chapter 3 on content analysis.

2.3.4 Languages

Both line 6 and line 14 are called "lang" and have conflicting values, which can be confusing. The first instance is the machine-detected language of the tweet's text itself. Twitter has algorithms that guess at what language the text is written in, based on alphabet and common dictionaries for each language.

This tends to be relatively accurate as far as major language differences go but can have issues with distinguishing between similar languages, and tends to err on the side of the more common language. For instance, the algorithm rarely mistakes English for Russian, but can frequently misclassify Ukrainian as Russian given the languages' similarities and the short samples of text it is working with. But this does mean that within a certain margin of error, you can easily and automatically identify the language of a tweet even if the user switches back and forth between different languages in different tweets.

On the other hand, line 14 indicates the language of the user, with a standard two-letter designation. So in this case, this user has set their device's language to Russian, while this particular tweet is clearly written in English.

One technical caveat is that while these two-letter language codes are the standard ISO 639-1 codes, there are some exceptions in which Twitter is apparently using a long-deprecated set of these codes. In particular, in 1988 there was a revision to the standard that changed the two-letter designation of a half-dozen languages. Twitter's language fields report the *old* two-letter designation for these languages for an unknown reason. The two most important such mismatches are Indonesian (reported as *in* although the correct code is *id*) and Hebrew (reported as *iw* instead of the modern *he*).

2.3.5 Times and Time Zones

First, the "created_at" field gives a time stamp for when the tweet was posted to Twitter. This is *always* in GMT, so you don't have to worry about time zone conversions to figure out when tweets were posted. If you download tweets from around the world, their timestamps will be compatible.

On the other hand, time zones of tweets can cause additional complications. While some researchers have used the time zone (defined in line 13 of the sample tweet) to great effect as a way to evaluate whether a particular tweeter is doing so from within a particular country or from elsewhere in the world, the data can have some issues. For example, Table 2.1 reports data for that same Euromaidan time period for Ukrainian users that we discussed in Section 2.3.4. The most popular setting by far is no setting at all, while the Kiev time zone that we would expect most Ukrainians to have their phones set to only manages a bit more than 10% of the total. As such, be very careful using the time zone field.

2.3.6 Entities

Finally, the object called "entities" contains a set of array objects that contain additional data about the tweet. The primary ones used are listed from lines 20 to 23, with the "..." simply a placeholder for the contents of these arrays, each of which has its own complicated structure that we will discuss in more detail when we use each of those objects for applications throughout the book. In summary though, the Twitter API provides convenient lists here of all the hashtags that appear in the tweet, any URLs, mentions of other users, and inclusions of media (such as images or video).

Table 2.1 Time zones of Ukrainian tweets during Euromaidan

# Users	% Users	Time Zone
121 132	45.2%	[Blank]
28 734	10.8%	Kyiv
21 512	8.0%	Moscow
15 545	5.8%	Quito
14 824	5.5%	Baghdad
13 417	5.0%	Abu Dhabi
11 830	4.4%	Athens
6 576	2.5%	Bucharest
5 231	2.0%	Greenland
3 220	1.2%	Minsk

2.4 Downloading Twitter Data

In this section, we will implement a basic Twitter data collection project using several different methods. These are very basic tools, but in later chapters, we will implement more complicated and specific applications of data collection and analysis for different sorts of research requirements.

For the purposes of this book, all code is written to be as simple and self-contained as possible, using external libraries only when necessary. The reason for this is to make the code as easy to understand as possible, while also making it simple for programmers from all backgrounds to modify the code for their own purposes. Often this means that the code will use less parsimonious constructs in order to be more transparent, if less optimized.

All code in this book has been written in Python 3, except for a few noted exceptions, and the sample projects share a great deal of structure that allows both consistency for different applications, and the ability for researchers to modify the code without having to invent their own structure.[3] That is, the code in this book is from real projects, using real data, and avoids wherever possible "toy" examples that don't scale outside their immediate context. All source code is available on the GitHub repository associated with this book, but sample code is also presented in the text itself to walk through the examples and how they

---

[3] For the most part the code should work with minor syntax tweaks in Python 2 if that is preferred in a particular research environment.

work. There are a couple of steps you need to take in order to get the code up and running.

2.4.1 A Framework for Data Collection

It is important to separate social media data collection into two components: the downloading of the data and the processing of that data into something usable for your research purposes. Most basic tutorials violate this separation in order to create simpler working examples. For instance, tutorials on accessing the Twitter API tend to have a bit of code that connects to the API, a for loop that iterates over the tweets that are downloaded, and a bit of code inside that for loop that does something with each tweet (like extracting its latitude and longitude, or checking to see if it contains a hashtag of interest, or any number of more sophisticated bits of logic). The tutorials will note that this specific spot inside the for loop is where the logic for your research project should be inserted. Similar techniques abound when setting up web scraping of blogs or other social media.

Instead, when designing a research project that involves social media data collection, one should separate at every level from the very beginning downloading from processing and analysis. The downloader should have the minimal complexity necessary to grab the desired data, and save it as unchanged as possible into local files for later processing. There are several reasons for this strict separation.

First and foremost is the issue of replicability, which is of paramount importance to social scientists. If the data returned by the search or web scraping changes after you initially do your research then there is no capacity for replicating the particular results that you generated. Real-world examples of this are quite common and are not easily dismissible edge cases. For instance, if the entire blog site in question is taken down and its archives are no longer publicly available your work is no longer replicable. If users (or governments) go back and modify the contents of social media after the fact, your work is no longer replicable. If you are using Twitter's API, as we discuss in Section 2.4.6, your work is no longer replicable if you are using either the streaming API or if more than seven days have passed since your initial downloads. By having exactly the data that you downloaded available at any time down the road for reuse, your research is inherently more replicable.

In addition to the basic scientific imperative of replicability though are a number of other more mundane concerns. First is the simple fact that while downloading is relatively easy to get right, analyzing data tends to be an iterative process of figuring out the best approach via trial and error. And even once you have your analysis code working perfectly, there is *always* another idea months down the road of different ways to approach the data if only for the sake of robustness checks. So long as you have your set corpus of downloaded data, you can modify your analysis as much as you like without having to depend on redownloading data over and over again with each change to your approach.

That brings up the additional concern of why redownloading is a problem, even beyond the replicability issues. Except for very small projects, downloading data en masse is resource intensive and tends to take significant time. For instance, if you are scraping blog entries that match a certain set of keywords, and have set up a downloader to politely only hit their server once per second (if only so that their systems don't ban your IP address), it will still take *weeks* to download that data if you have millions of results.

Download using a wide net, and do so exactly one time. Even for the simplest social media data projects, I have a minimum of two programs running as part of the project, written in whatever programming language is appropriate: *grab* that does the downloading and saving, and *process* that does everything else, but does so operating on the downloaded files so it can be run repeatedly with different settings. Larger and more complex projects work with the same basic design, although as they become more and more complicated, the *process* program often becomes split into many different ones as analysis becomes richer. But the separation of downloading from processing remains intact at all times.

2.4.2 Getting Set Up

In order to use Twitter's API, you need to first set up a normal Twitter account. If you already have an account with Twitter, you can make use of that one, or you can set up a new one just for this work. There's no need to use the account to actually post to Twitter: I downloaded over three billion tweets before posting my first tweet, which may be a record if anyone is keeping track of such things.

After you have a Twitter account, go to https://developer.twitter.com, login, and then go into the Apps section and click the appropriate button to create a new app. You can name it anything you like, but it's typical to simply name your app after whatever your main project is. Follow the instructions and you will be given four long alphanumeric strings that are needed to authenticate yourself with the Twitter API via code.[4] Those are called the consumer_key, consumer_secret, access_token, and access_token_secret. The details of these strings are not particularly important, but copy and paste them somewhere easy for you to reference. In addition, I highly recommend you apply to Twitter for the elevation of your developer account to Academic tier. This is free, but

---

[4] These instructions are intentionally vague in order to not become obsolete the moment Twitter happens to redesign the webpages in question.

provides a great deal more functionality, and higher limits on the number of tweets you can download.

You also will need to install a minimal number of additional libraries for Python to use for this project that are not necessarily installed by default. Those libraries are NumPy (a scientific computing package), Pandas (a data analysis library), SQLite3 (a database library), and TweePy (a library for accessing the Twitter API). These are common and mature packages and should be easily installable using Pip (the Python package manager). Several additional packages will be required for specific applications later in the book, but these four are foundational.

Next, download the source code for all examples from this book's associated website (hosted at `https://github.com/slwilson4/smassd`). There is a top-level directory that contains two files: *my_settings.py* and *smassd_functions.py*. The latter contains some helper functions and should be left alone, while the former contains a set of currently empty variables where you will need to copy and paste in your specific keys for the Twitter application you set up two paragraphs ago. That file is displayed in Snippet 2.2 and the empty strings are where your application codes should be inserted.

Once you set up your Twitter application, install the requisite libraries, and modify *my_settings.py*, all the rest of the code in this section should run for you without modification, although we will walk through how it all works.

Throughout this book, I provide full source code examples so that it is easy to follow along with the *logic* of implementation while reading. However, for actual deployment and customization of any of the code, I expect that most users should start from the code provided by the GitHub repository rather than individually typing the code from the text of the book. In my experience, books that include the code as comprehensively as possible in the text are easier to follow the logic of, even if at face value all that computer code seems rendered moot by the provision of electronic copies of the code. While the use of abbreviated samples of code or pseudocode might be superficially easier to read, it is much harder to follow the complete logic of the implemented code. Ideally, the text will be used in conjunction with the code, rather than either existing in a vacuum.

Also in the top-level directory of the book's source code, you should see a number of sub-directories, each of which is descriptively named. The "Classes" folder contains code that is used across multiple applications, while the numbered directories are example applications. Each of these directories is a self-contained and fully functional data collection and processing project. In addition, each has a similar base structure so that the logic in each is easy to follow. First, there is a file called *snag.py* that downloads and collects raw JSON from Twitter. Second, there is a directory called *queues* that stores those raw JSON files

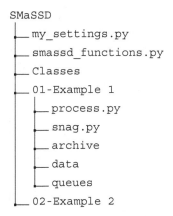

```
SMaSSD
├── my_settings.py
├── smassd_functions.py
├── Classes
├── 01-Example 1
│   ├── process.py
│   ├── snag.py
│   ├── archive
│   ├── data
│   └── queues
└── 02-Example 2
```

Figure 2.1 Basic directory structure of projects

(because that it is where they are queued up to be processed). Third, there is a file called *process.py* that opens files in the queues directory, and performs some type of operation on each tweet. Fourth, there is a directory called *archive* that stores JSON files that have already been processed. Fifth, there is a directory called *data* into which *process.py* will save all postprocessed data. This basic structure varies from project to project as additional functionality is added, but the fundamental logic remains and is summarized in Figure 2.1.

```
1 consumer_key=""
2 consumer_secret=""
3 access_token=""
4 access_token_secret=""
```

Code Snippet 2.2 Application settings

2.4.3 A Basic Downloader

For a first project we will set up a basic system for taking a list of existing tweet ids, and downloading the full data for each tweet. This is a useful exercise because of the plethora of available replication datasets that are simply lists of unique identifiers of tweets that fit a certain category. For example, Harvard Dataverse currently hosts a number of such projects including the unique ids for all tweets by members of the 115th Congress while in office (Littman, 2017) or tweets relating to the Irish 8th amendment referendum (Littman, 2018). This sort of replication strategy is designed to comply with the terms of use for the Twitter API, which forbids the public redistribution of the *content* of tweets beyond a certain unusefully low number.

The code below (Snippet 2.3) is the first few lines of *snag.py* for our first project. This includes all of the import commands in order to give it access to the appropriate libraries and packages. These 22 lines of code are at the start of all the files from here on, but for parsimony, I leave them off in the text of the book except where adding new libraries for specific applications.

```
 1  # general libraries used
 2  import sys
 3  import pprint
 4  import json
 5  import re
 6  import os
 7  import shutil
 8  import codecs
 9  import time
10
11  # specific libraries used
12  import numpy as np
13  import pandas as pd
14  import tweepy
15  from tweepy import *
16  import sqlite3
17
18  # including the SMaSSD support files
19  sys.path.append("../Classes/")
20  sys.path.append("..")
21  from smassd_functions import *
22  from my_settings import *
```

Code Snippet 2.3 Library and package loading

Next is the main body of the code (Snippet 2.4), which takes an existing list of tweet ids and downloads and saves all data about those tweets. Line 2 establishes the input file, where the code can find the tweet ids. It is a sample CSV file that lists the tweet ids for 50 of Alexandria Ocasio-Cortez's tweets from early 2019, but any other list of such ids could be substituted in its place. Line 3 tells the program where to save the full data of those tweets once it acquires them, in this case to what will be our standard target, a file in the queues directory. Lines 6 through 8 set up a simple Python array of the tweet ids, populating them using a Pandas data frame, which has some helpful functionality in terms of dealing with CSV files. Lines 11 through 13 connect to the Twitter API using the codes specific to your application that you set up earlier, and generally should not need modified in any of the subsequent programs.

The next chunk of code (lines 16 through 25) actually retrieves the tweet data from Twitter. It sets up an empty array to store the data, and then loops through each of the ids loaded before. The actual call to the Twitter API is wrapped in a try/except construct in order to ensure that an error retrieving a single tweet doesn't crash the entire process, while printing to the console which tweet id caused the problem. Lines 19 through 22 use the *get_status* function from TweePy to download a single tweet. The two parameters we pass in addition to the id itself are important to understand. First, line 21's "tweet_mode='extended'" tells the API that you want the full text of the tweet instead of the abbreviated 140-character version that is the default for backward compatibility. Second, line 22's "wait_on_rate_limit=True" tells the program to pay attention to your account's current allowed quota of hits against the API. For example, Twitter sets a limit of 900 hits to the *get_status* function per 15-minute period per account. If you exceed that, Twitter will send back an error message instead of the tweet data. In extreme cases of exceeding quotas, your account can be automatically suspended. Essentially this flag just tells your program to check if you're at the rate limit, and if so, to wait a few minutes until your quota refreshes. Finally, line 23 appends the returned tweet data to the output array.

The last few lines of the program (lines 28–32) open the output file specified on line 3 and use the JSON library to save each tweet's data to its own line in the file. This is a standard JSON file that can be opened by a text editor or a web browser, or imported into a variety of other programs if you like. It contains many more fields and much more structure than we will typically use in any given application, but by saving the *entire* output, we can keep our options open for the use of that data in different ways down the road.

```
1  # Variable definitions
2  inputFile = "input.csv"
3  outputFile = "queues/output.json"
4
5  # Grab list of tweet IDs to download
6  ids = []
7  df = pd.read_csv(inputFile,encoding='UTF-8')
8  ids = [x for x in df['id']]
9
10 # Connect to API
11 auth_handler = OAuthHandler(consumer_key,consumer_secret)
12 auth_handler.set_access_token(access_token,access_token_secret)
13 api = API(auth_handler)
14
15 # Loop through IDs and download them
16 tweets = []
17 for id in ids:
18     try:
19         tweet = api.get_status(
20                     id,
21                     tweet_mode='extended',
22                     wait_on_rate_limit=True)
23         tweets.append(tweet)
```

```
24      except:
25          log("Error downloading tweet: "+str(id))
26
27  # Write tweets to file
28  file = open(outputFile, 'w', encoding='UTF-8')
29  for tweet in tweets:
30      json.dump(tweet._json, file)
31      file.write("\n")
32  file.close()
33  log("Finished")
```

Code Snippet 2.4 Basic tweet downloader

2.4.4 A Basic Processor

Next, we set up a basic processor for taking any number of downloaded tweets in JSON form and applying our own project's logic to them. The code for this basic processor is detailed in Snippet 2.5.

The first few lines (2–5) initialize some useful variables for the rest of the program. Notice that the *inputJSON* variable corresponds to the file output by the *snag.py* program we wrote in Section 2.4.3. Lines 8 through 21 are the function that will process each tweet, the logic of which we'll return to in a moment. The main body of the program starts on line 24 and is primarily composed of opening the input JSON file and then looping through each line of it. Line 26 strips out any new line characters stuck at the end of the JSON, while the next couple of lines define a pair of variables to track what is happening. We cast the line from our input file into a JSON object that Python can appropriately handle on line 32, however, note that we also wrap that process in a try/catch statement so that if the line happens to be invalid JSON the program can just skip that line and move on to the next tweet. This logic isn't strictly necessary, but when scaling this application up to streaming thousands or millions of tweets, a bit of malformed JSON in an occasional tweet is one of the most common problems that will cause code to error out.

After ensuring the JSON of this specific tweet is loaded, line 37 then calls our processing function defined up on line 8. If the function returns a proper response, the processed version of the tweet is appended to our array of tweets to output on line 39.

The processing function itself is relatively straightforward in this case. Line 10 loads the text of the tweet and then strips out any new line characters or tabs in order to make it tidier to deal with in a CSV file. Then lines 12 through 18 create a Python dictionary pulling out specific fields that we might be interested in. In this case, we are pulling out a very simple set of the fields defined in the Twitter API. Just the text of the tweet, the tweet's unique id, the screen name of the user, the user's unique id, and the time stamp at which the tweet was posted. Different projects will require the extraction of different data from the tweet's metadata, and so this *processTweet* function can be adapted to pull whatever fields are of interest. For instance, in a project where location matters, extracting and processing the geocode object would be of importance. In network analysis, extracting the number of followers the user had at the time of the tweet might be important. Notice that the "created" field runs a helper function called *processTimestamp* from the book's functions file that simply converts the Twitter formatted time stamp into a more standard one recognized by databases and spreadsheets.

Also note that once again we are wrapping some logic with a try/except statement. In this case, we are catching a *KeyError*, which means that one of the fields we tried to pull out of the JSON wasn't actually found. Occasionally, the downloader will store a tweet that technically has validly formatted JSON (and thus it passes the previous error check) but is still malformed enough that it is inconsistent with the other tweets. Again, this is a rare occurrence that the sheer scale of big data can turn into a commonly encountered problem.

The last two lines cast the processed tweets into a Pandas data frame that is then written to a CSV file. At this point you have a basic downloading infrastructure set up and ready to go!

```
1  # Variable definitions
2  inputJSON = "queues/output.json"
3  outputCSV = "data/output.csv"
4  columns = ['id', 'created', 'user_id', 'screen_name', 'text']
5  output_tweets = []
6
7
8  # The function to process an individual tweet
9  def processTweet(a):
10     try:
11         text = a['full_text'].replace('\n', ' ')
12         text = text.replace('\r', '').replace('\t', ' ')
13         timestamp = procTimestamp(a['created_at'])
14         ret = {
15             'id': a['id'],
16             'created': timestamp,
17             'user_id': a['user']['id'],
18             'screen_name': a['user']['screen_name'],
19             'text': text
20         }
21         return ret
```

```
22      except KeyError:
23          return False
24
25
26 # Open JSON file and process each tweet
27 infile = codecs.open(inputJSON, "r", "utf-8")
28 for line in infile:
29     line.rstrip("\n")
30     tweet_json = False
31     tweet_processed = False
32
33     # Catch whether the line is properly formed JSON, else skip
34     try:
35         tweet_json = json.loads(line)
36     except ValueError:
37         tweet_json = False
38
39     if tweet_json:
40         tweet_processed = processTweet(tweet_json)
41     if tweet_processed:
42         output_tweets.append(tweet_processed)
43
44 infile.close()
45
46 # Write those tweets to a CSV file
47 output_tweets_pd = pd.DataFrame(output_tweets)
48 output_tweets_pd.to_csv(outputCSV, index=False)
```

Code Snippet 2.5 Basic tweet processor

2.4.5 Adding a Database Backend

While CSV files are convenient for small projects, they are very limited when scaling projects to larger sizes, or when needing to do additional operations on already processed data. For instance, let's say that we used the previous system to download all tweets posted by members of Congress during the 2016–2018 congressional term. That amounts to nearly 1.5 million tweets, which is generally speaking going to be too large to effectively do anything with in Excel or similar programs. Further, if we want to do operations on the data after the fact, CSV files are not well-suited for being opened and systematically modified. For instance, if we wanted to extract only the tweets that were posted during the few weeks leading up to an election and flag any that use particular keywords, we could certainly modify our *process.py* script to do so, but it's an unnecessarily complicated operation. Big data calls for databases, because the size and complexity of social media data projects simply requires more functionality than can be managed by keeping data stored in CSV or JSON files directly on the hard drive.

As such, throughout the book, where appropriate we will use SQLite databases, which are a very simple but efficient flat file database system. Experienced programmers can adapt this over to Postgres, MySQL, Oracle, or other more robust database environments, but SQLite offers an efficient and highly transportable solution that works on any operating system users of the book might be using and can easily be manipulated with a graphical interface without requiring the installation of additional software.

Snippet 2.6 shows how to create a basic SQLite database with fields that match those we are extracting in our basic processing script. Line 3 specifies the file path and name of the database that we want to create. In our case, we are just creating a file called *output.db* in the same directory where we previously saved our CSV output file. Lines 5–11 make up the command that creates a new table called *tweets* in this database. The lower-case words on lines 6 through 10 are the names of the columns we are creating (which should look familiar from Section 2.4.4) while the all-caps words are the type of data we are going to store in each field. The two id fields are BIGINT (i.e. "big integer"), and the two text fields are VARCHAR (which means "variable characters," but in simple terms just means that text goes in these fields). Finally, *created* is a "DATETIME" field, which tells the database that an exact date and time goes in this field. The need to specify the sort of data going into each field is so that powerful search functions can be used to query the data, such as date ranges on the "created" field or regular expressions on the text fields. If you want to modify this to store different data from the tweets you are processing, this file can be modified by adding additional fields with appropriate data types, which we will do on many occasions throughout the book. Finally, line 12 specifies that the id field of the tweet is a unique field, to ensure that duplicates of the same tweets aren't entered.

```
1  import sqlite3
2
3  conn = sqlite3.connect("data/data.db")
4  c = conn.cursor()
5  c.execute('''CREATE TABLE tweets (
6              id BIGINT,
7              created DATETIME,
8              text VARCHAR,
9              user_id BIGINT,
10             screen_name VARCHAR
11             )''')
12 c.execute('''CREATE UNIQUE INDEX idx_id ON tweets(id)''')
13 conn.commit()
14 conn.close()
```

Code Snippet 2.6 Creating a SQLite database

Next, we adopt a technique called *object-oriented programming* that adds a little complexity but a lot of power. In this case, we define a new object type called *BasicTweet* that has attributes like the tweet id or user's screen name, and functions for doing things like inserting into the database or processing the data in new and interesting ways without us having to cut and paste that code into every subsequent processor that we write for different applications.

The *BasicTweet* object is defined in a separate file called *BasicTweet.py* that is in the classes directory at the top level of the project's source code. This is because we use that same code for a variety of the applications in the book (and if you open that file you will see a lot of additional code that we use later in the book for different applications). The source code of this object is rendered in Snippet 2.7. It is is comprised of two methods (which is what functions are called in an object-oriented framework): _ _init_ _ and *insert*. The former is a special method (hence the odd name with underscores in it) that all objects have. The technical name for it is a *constructor*, which simply means a method used to initially set up (or *construct*) a new instance of this object. The variable "s" throughout these object files stands for "self," meaning that it is talking about a variable attached specifically to itself. So "s.json" refers to a variable called "json" specifically associated with this particular instance of a tweet, "s.tweet_id" refers to the unique id of this specific tweet, and so on.

Lines 5 through 14 set up a tweet object by taking in the JSON like we've done before, and processing it so we can use the data. We have added a field called "valid," which makes it easy to check if each tweet was able to be correctly processed. Lines 16 through 24 are the "insert" method, which very simply creates an array called "q" that lists the data we want to insert, and then inserts it with the SQL command in lines 21 through 24. The question marks indicate where items from a list should be inserted in the order they appear in "q."

```
1  class BasicTweet:
2      def __init__(s, json):
3          s.json = json
4          s.valid = True
5          try:
6              s.tweet_id = json['id']
7              if 'text' in json:
8                  s.text = json['text']
9              if 'full_text' in json:
10                 s.text = json['full_text']
11             if 'extended_tweet' in json:
12                 if 'full_text' in json['extended_tweet']:
13                     s.text = json['extended_tweet']['full_text']
14             s.text = s.text.replace('\n', ' ')
15             s.text = s.text.replace('\r', '')
16             s.text = s.text.replace('\t', ' ')
```

```
17          s.created = procTimestamp(json['created_at'])
18          s.user_id = json['user']['id']
19          s.screen_name = json['user']['screen_name']
20      except KeyError:
21          s.valid = False
22
23  def insert(s, c):
24      q = (
25          s.tweet_id, s.created, s.user_id,
26          s.screen_name, s.text
27      )
28      c.execute("""REPLACE INTO tweets
29          (id, created, user_id, screen_name, text)
30          VALUES(?,?,?,?,?)""", q)
```

Code Snippet 2.7 Basic tweet object

Snippet 2.8 details the script *process_db.py*, which is similar in structure to the *process.py* program we created in Section 2.4.4. There are a couple of minor changes to note that will be important in later examples as well. First, we tell it how to get to *BasicTweet* using the command on line 2 that tells it to import that class. Second, in line 3 we specify the database file we just created instead of the CSV file from Section 2.4.4. The same basic functionality of looping through the tweets in the JSON file and processing them is retained but now we do so utilizing the *BasicTweet* code that we wrote in Snippet 2.7. So in line 21, for each tweet we create (or "instantiate") a *BasicTweet* object using the JSON for that tweet (this is automatically passed to the *__init__* method). Finally, in the last few lines of the code, we now connect to the database (with very similar commands to the database creation script) and then loop through all of the tweets and insert each individually using the *insert* method from *BasicTweet*.

```
1  # Variable definitions
2  from BasicTweet import BasicTweet
3  inputJSON = "queues/output.json"
4  outputDB = "data/data.db"
5  tweets = []
6
7  # Open JSON file and process each tweet
8  infile = codecs.open(inputJSON, "r", "utf-8")
9  for line in infile:
10     line.rstrip("\n")
11     tweet_json = False
12     tweet_processed = None
13
14     # Catch whether the line is properly formed JSON, else skip
15     try:
16         tweet_json = json.loads(line)
```

```
17    except ValueError:
18        tweet_json = False
19
20    if tweet_json:
21        tweet_processed = BasicTweet(tweet_json)
22        if tweet_processed.valid:
23            tweets.append(tweet_processed)
24 infile.close()
25
26 # Write those tweets to a database file
27 conn = sqlite3.connect(outputDB)
28 c = conn.cursor()
29 for tweet in tweets:
30    tweet.insert(c)
31 conn.commit()
32 conn.close()
```

Code Snippet 2.8 Basic tweet processor with database

You can use various graphical interfaces in order to access the data stored in SQLite databases, or of course you can write additional Python scripts to manipulate the data directly, which we will do a lot of in the course of the book. For the purposes of taking quick graphical looks at the data, a good piece of software is *SQLite DB Browser* (available free for all major operating systems at http:// sqlitebrowser.org). This will allow you spreadsheet-style access to databases much larger than anything typical spreadsheet software can support, along with the ability to query the data using SQL. An excellent tutorial that walks through how to write your own queries and really leverage the advantages of databases can be found online here: www.sqlitetutorial.net.

2.4.6 Processing Multiple Files

In practice, projects will likely acquire many more than a single JSON file full of tweets, especially streaming projects that continuously download more data over time. In this section, we set up a more advanced version of the processor from Section 2.4.5 that should be robust enough to handle this for most of the subsequent projects in the book, with only minor modifications. Snippet 2.9 shows the file called *process_all.py*, which takes the essential logic of *process_db.py* from Section 2.4.5, but adds some critical features.

```
1 # Variable definitions
2 from BasicTweet import BasicTweet
3 inputDir = "queues/"
4 archiveDir = "archive/"
5 database = "data/data.db"
6 tweets = []
7
```

```
 8  # Loop through each file and process its tweets
 9  for filename in os.listdir(inputDir):
10      if filename.endswith(".json"):
11          inputJSON = inputDir+filename
12          archiveJSON = archiveDir+filename
13          # Open JSON file and process each tweet
14          infile = codecs.open(inputJSON, "r","utf-8")
15          for line in infile:
16              line.rstrip("\n")
17              tweet_json = False
18              tweet_processed = None
19
20              # Catch whether the line is properly formed JSON, else skip
21              try:
22                  tweet_json = json.loads(line)
23              except ValueError:
24                  tweet_json = False
25
26              if tweet_json:
27                  tweet_processed = BasicTweet(tweet_json)
28                  if tweet_processed:
29                      tweets.append(tweet_processed)
30          infile.close()
31          os.rename(inputJSON, archiveJSON)
32
33  # Write those tweets to a database file
34  conn = sqlite3.connect(database)
35  c = conn.cursor()
36  for tweet in tweets:
37      tweet.insert(c)
38  conn.commit()
39  conn.close()
```

Code Snippet 2.9 Advanced tweet processor with database and archiving

Rather than taking as an input a single JSON file, this program instead loops through all of the JSON files in the *queues* subdirectory. This is accomplished on lines 9 and 10, which loop through the files in that input directory, and check to see if they're a JSON file before proceeding. Lines 14 through 30 are identical to the core logic of *process_db.py*, validating the file's contents and processing them through the *BasicTweet* class. The only addition is line 31, which moves each processed JSON file over to the *archive* directory. The latter is done so that the same JSON files aren't processed over and over again.

This program, in conjunction with the *snag.py* program, constitutes the fundamental functionality of most of the rest of the book. A program downloads JSON files to the queues directory, and another program loops through those files, processes the tweets, inserts them into a database, and then archives the JSON file. Adding functionality, such as wanting additional fields pulled from each tweet, can be accomplished by either adding methods to the *BasicTweet* object or by creating a new class and using that instead.

2.4.7 Collecting a Worldwide Sample

The previous examples relied on knowing the unique ids of particular tweets from an external source, so next we are going to set up some original data collection using Twitter's API. In this case, the simplest application to set up is also one of the largest data collection efforts possible. One of the connection points that Twitter makes available through the streaming API is the "sample," which is simply a 1% random sample of *all* tweets at any given time. We are going to set up the code to connect to and download that entire stream.

This is an enormous amount of data, totaling approximately 5–6 million tweets on the average day, or about a quarter million tweets per hour with some variance throughout the course of the day as peak hours for parts of the world wax and wane. In terms of disk size, which is perhaps a little easier to wrap one's mind around usefully, this is about 20 gigabytes of JSON downloads per day.

From a certain perspective, it's impressive just how *small* this figure is. Streaming content in HD from Netflix will use about 3 gigabytes per hour of bandwidth, and the download of a recent video game via Steam will often be in the ballpark of 50–100 gigabytes. That is, a decent home internet connection is perfectly capable of handling the bandwidth necessary to download 1% of all tweets in the world in real time. On the other hand, this is a figure that grows staggeringly large when you consider collecting over the long term, adding up quickly into many terabytes of data.

Snippet 2.10 shows a new class called *Streamer* that we will use to handle the basics of downloading from the streaming API both here and in later examples that make use of keyword and geographic filters. Lines 3 through 10 are the function *initQueue*, which sets up and opens a new JSON file to which we'll be saving tweets. It takes as inputs three values: *output_dir* (the directory you want to save these files to), *rotation_time* (how many seconds each file should be used before creating a new one), and *label* (a prefix for the created file so that if we have multiple streamers we can tell their files apart). Line 8 saves the current time, and line 9 creates a file using those parameters plus the current time stamp. Line 9 creates a new file, with a name prefaced by the input label, and the current time stamp turned into a readable form that will nonetheless have the advantage of being in chronological order when sorted alphabetically.

```
1  class Streamer(tweepy.StreamListener):
2
3      def initQueue(s, output_dir, rotation_time, label):
4          s.output_dir = output_dir
5          s.rotation_time = rotation_time
6          s.label = label
7          # create new output file
8          s.last_rotated = datetime.datetime.now()
```

```
 9        s.file_name = s.label+'_'+f'{s.last_rotated:%Y%m%d-%H%M%S}'+'.json'
10        s.file = open(s.output_dir+'/'+s.file_name, 'w', encoding='UTF-8')
11
12    def on_status(s, tweet):
13        current_time = datetime.datetime.now()
14        time_elapsed = (current_time - s.last_rotated).seconds
15        if time_elapsed>s.rotation_time:
16            s.file.close()
17            s.initQueue(s.output_dir, s.rotation_time, s.label)
18        json.dump(tweet._json, s.file)
19        s.file.write("\n")
```

Code Snippet 2.10 Streamer object

The function *on_status* runs every single time a tweet comes down the stream. It serves to check what the current time is, checks to see if the time elapsed since the last rotation has exceed the set time for rotation, and if so closes the old file and runs *initQueue* to set up a new one. The reason for this rotation of files is so that any given file doesn't get too large to handle and we can process old files while new ones are being downloaded. It then writes the tweet to the current JSON file on lines 18 and 19. This Streamer object should serve well enough for all your needs for the rest of the book and should not need to be modified very often in your own applications.

Snippet 2.11 shows the actual downloader (from *snag_sample.py*). On line 1, it imports the Streamer object we just set up, and then on lines 6 through 8 sets up the connection to the Twitter API as we have done with previous downloaders. In lines 10 and 11 we initialize the Streamer object we just described, and then call the *initQueue* function. Line 13 is a built-in function that tells the stream to grab the 1% random sample of tweets.

For example, with an output directory of "queues," a rotation time of 3 600 seconds (i.e. one hour), and a label of "sample," if we run this code at 17 seconds after 8:30 in the morning on February 1, 2019 then it would create a file called "sample_20190201_083017.json" in the queues directory, and save tweets in it for an hour, at which point it would switch to another file called "sample_20190201_093017.json."

```
1  from Streamer import Streamer
2
3  # Variable definitions
4  output_dir = "queues"
5
6  auth_handler = OAuthHandler(consumer_key, consumer_secret)
7  auth_handler.set_access_token(access_token, access_token_secret)
8  api = API(auth_handler)
9
```

```
10 | listener = Streamer()
11 | listener.initQueue(output_dir, 3600, 'sample')
12 | stream = tweepy.Stream(auth=api.auth, listener=listener)
13 | stream.sample()
```

Code Snippet 2.11 Downloading sample of all tweets worldwide

Those few lines of code are all you require in order to start downloading a 1% random sample of all communication in the world on Twitter, in real time. Given enough disk space to store it all, you have now entered the world of big data.

2.4.8 Compressing Data

The sheer size of social media data being downloaded en masse means that disk space inevitably becomes a precious commodity. However, the data being downloaded is quite amenable to being heavily compressed to ease the burden of storage. Snippet 2.12 is a simple program that is a modified version of our previous processor programs that compresses each JSON file in a specified directory using standard zip files that any operating system should be able to open when needed. Note that on line 7, the program loops through each JSON file in a directory as we have done previously, and on line 10 it creates a zip file of the same name as the JSON file (except with .zip instead of .json as a suffix) and stores it in a directory called "zipped."

```
1 | # Variable definitions
2 | import zipfile
3 | inputDir = "archive/"
4 | zippedDir = "zipped/"
5 |
6 | # Loop through each file and compress it
7 | for filename in os.listdir(inputDir):
8 |     if filename.endswith(".json"):
9 |         inputFile = inputDir+filename
10 |         outputFile = zippedDir+filename.replace('json','zip')
11 |         zippedArchive = zipfile.ZipFile(outputFile, 'w',
12 |                                 compression=zipfile.ZIP_DEFLATED)
13 |         zippedArchive.write(inputFile, compress_type = zipfile.ZIP_DEFLATED)
14 |         zippedArchive.close()
```

Code Snippet 2.12 Compressing JSON files

The end result is a zip file for each JSON file, which tends to compress by about six times. That is, the resultant zip file is about a sixth the size of the JSON file.[5] If used in conjunction with the 1% sample stream of Section 2.4.7, that

---

[5] This code can be told to use other compression schemes such as LZMA that can compress JSON up to twice as much as the zip algorithm, but I have opted to use the more standard zip file format in the text because of its familiar use.

means our long-term data requirements would not be 20 gigabytes per day, but only about 3.5 gigabytes.

2.5 Conclusion

This chapter only touches on the broad strokes of the enormous amount of data available on Twitter, and sets up the foundation for how to download and process that data. In the next few chapters we will discuss applications for analyzing that data from a variety of methodological perspectives.

3 Content Analysis of Social Media Data

This is the first of three chapters that each focus on a particular method for analyzing social media data. *Content*, as a broad rubric, constitutes one of the most exciting parts of using social media as a data source. For the first time in history, normal people around the world have the capacity for mass communication that was once reserved only for elites. The content of that communication, the meanings and concepts that billions of people are choosing to use their voices for in this new electronic medium, is perhaps the most essential and novel element of this new source of data. And while social media has democratized the ability of individuals to communicate, it has also democratized the process of research, by putting the tools to analyze that massive source of communication in the hands of social science researchers. In this chapter, we will first summarize the variety and scale of content available on social media, introduce some additional data collection techniques to account for the data needs that revolve around content analysis projects, and then walk through a number of content analysis techniques applied to social media data.

3.1 Text and Twitter

The text available for analysis on social media is deceptively simple. Even limited to 140 (or 280) characters, the sheer scope of text from every corner of the globe yields a proliferation of corner cases, exceptions to every rule, and challenges to researchers trying to extract specific data. Take for instance the simple question of what language a tweet is written in.

Because social media is a worldwide phenomenon, dozens of languages are represented on it to one degree or another. Recall from Chapter 2 that two different language fields are available in Twitter data: the language setting of the user on their device and the machine-detected language of each tweet.

Table 3.1 shows the top 20 machine-detected languages of tweets. Note that English is by far the modal language on Twitter, representing some 36% of total tweets. This is due to a number of factors, including English's status as something of a lingua franca online, and the relatively higher proportion of Twitter users who reside in the United States. While different social media sites will vary in

Table 3.1 Language breakdown of tweets globally

Rank	Language	% of Tweets
1	English	36.1%
2	Portuguese	14.1%
3	Unknown	10.5%
4	Spanish	10.4%
5	Japanese	5.6%
6	Indonesian	4.6%
7	Arabic	3.7%
8	Tagalog	2.8%
9	Turkish	2.7%
10	French	1.7%
11	Hindi	1.2%
12	Thai	0.8%
13	Italian	0.8%
14	Russian	0.7%
15	Dutch	0.5%
16	German	0.5%
17	Haitian	0.3%
18	Polish	0.3%
19	Catalan	0.2%
20	Korean	0.2%

their precise language breakdown, English's modality is a common feature on sites that originated in the Western world.

However, note that the third most commonly identified language is simply "unknown," that is, the language detection algorithm was unable to identify a language for a full 10% of tweets. This is an inevitable consequence of the exceptionally short nature of the text in tweets, which often are composed of nothing more than a word or two that might be from any number of related languages. Or, even more simply, consider how many tweets are some variation on a cut-and-pasted URL and a smiley face emoticon.

Portuguese and Spanish hold up the next two slots, due to the overwhelming usage of social media in general and Twitter in particular in Latin America (far more so than Spain and Portugal in sheer quantity). After that, there is a mix of languages from around the world, with Turkish and Arabic from the Middle East, a number of East Asian languages, and the balance of common Western

European languages. All told, the top twenty languages represent over 95% of all tweets, and the top five 75%.

Note the absence of Chinese from this list despite the vast internet-connected population of China. Chinese comes in at #22, between Estonian and Finnish. Twitter (along with most other Western social media) has been effectively blocked in China since 2009, although a small number of tweets do still originate from within the country. From geocoded tweets, we can see that about a third of Chinese-language tweets originate from Taiwan, while a further 10% come from the United States.

One might question whether using the user-defined language field would be more reliable than relying on machine detection of each tweet's language. However, that field has some nuance to it due to the way that it is populated and information we have about how people are setting up their phones historically in different contexts. In particular, the history of character limits on tweets informs the emergence of complications when dealing with tweets from countries without Latin alphabets. For example, Russia and other countries in the post-Soviet sphere have a fascinating history with text encoding in electronic devices that continues to impact data collected today. When SMS messaging first was introduced, it only worked with ASCII-encoded text, which is a very basic set of characters that only includes the Latin characters used in the Western world, along with numbers, punctuation, and a handful of accented characters. But this meant that when SMS messaging was imported into parts of the world that used different character sets (like Cyrillic), some strange behavior emerged in order to force it to work.

In the Russian-speaking world, rather than using a Cyrillic encoding (like KOI-8) engineers adapted cell phones to use Unicode (UTF-8) instead. This more universal encoding is on a technical level the simplest way to go about supporting multiple character sets, but was in this particular practice less than ideal because in order to accommodate all of the characters from different languages, the resultant text is several times larger in terms of number of bytes. And so when Russians typed in 140 characters in Cyrillic, it would then require on the backend several packets to send instead of exactly one. And in the era when people were charged per text message, this meant that sending texts in Cyrillic cost several times as much as sending texts in Latin characters.

This led to the Russian market selling phones that had both Cyrillic and Latin characters on the keys, and Russians sensibly would change their phone's language setting to "English" in order to send text messages, while just selecting the Latin characters that most resembled each Cyrillic character. This led to a sort of pidgin language of Russian typed with Latin characters called Volapuk. To this day it is something "everyone knows" in the Russian-speaking world that sending texts in Russian costs more money than those sent in English,

Table 3.2 Machine-detected vs. user-setting languages in Ukrainian tweets

	Machine-detected			User-setting	
#	Language	% Tweets	#	Language	% Tweets
1	Russian	80.4	1	Russian	58.8
2	Ukrainian	6.4	2	English	33.4
3	English	5.1	3	Ukrainian	1.8
4	Unknown	2.7	4	Turkish	1.7
5	Bulgarian	2.1	5	Romanian	0.9
6	Turkish	0.5	6	Spanish	0.8
7	Lithuanian	0.4	7	Polish	0.7
8	Spanish	0.3	8	Lithuanian	0.4
9	Arabic	0.2	9	French	0.3
10	German	0.2	10	German	0.2

despite it not actually having been the case for at least a decade now. In addition, the average Russian had little understanding of the technical reasons of text encoding, but the idea that imported American technology would punish Russians for speaking Russian seemed perfectly plausible.

A good illustration of this in action is to examine a specific language in detail. For example, see Table 3.2, which lists the most common machine-detected and user-defined languages of geocoded tweets from within Ukraine during the six-month period around the Euromaidan protests from 2013 to 2014.

Ukrainian, which one would naturally expect to be the modal language choice for a Ukrainian, represents less than 2% of the tweets according to the user settings, and only 6.4% according to machine detection of the tweet's language. A full third of tweets are from users who set their device's language to English, despite a tiny 5.1% of tweets actually being detected as being in English.

If one delves into the tweets themselves, the accuracy of these figures is thrown further into question. A significant portion of the tweets from the accounts set to English by their users are clearly Ukrainian (complete with Cyrillic characters), while the same is the case with the "Russian" tweets. In addition, many of the "Ukrainian" tweets are Russian language upon inspection. This is representing a disconnect between what the user's device is set to as its language and what language the user actually is typing in.

This anecdotal dive into Ukrainian and Russian serves to illustrate how when it comes to Twitter data, a scholar would do best to take the languages of tweets and users with a grain of salt. That is not to say the field should be ignored, but that the data is rich and complex and should be approached with constant validation checks to make sure that what you think you are capturing is what you are *actually* capturing.

3.1.1 Downloading Tweets by Keyword

One of the most common research designs for collecting social media data is to determine certain keywords of interest, and to download all tweets that contain that keyword. That functionality is relatively easy to set up by modifying the streamer that we set up in the last chapter.

Snippet 3.1 shows this modified processor, *snag_kw.py*. It broadly works the same way, with line 5 defining where the JSON files will be stored, lines 7–9 setting up authentication, and lines 11–14 starting the streamer itself. Note that on line 12 we change the "label" from "sample" to "kw" so that the JSON files will be prefixed with "kw" instead. On line 4, we set up an array that lists the keywords that we want to search for, and on line 14 we tell the streamer to just grab tweets with the words in that array. Note that line 14 calls *stream.filter()* instead of *stream.sample()*, which means that the search here will return *all* tweets in real time that match the selected keywords.

```
1  from Streamer import Streamer
2
3  # Variable definitions
4  keywords = ['corona', 'covid', 'health', '#pandemic', '@CDCgov']
5  output_dir = "queues"
6
7  auth_handler = OAuthHandler(consumer_key, consumer_secret)
8  auth_handler.set_access_token(access_token, access_token_secret)
9  api = API(auth_handler)
10
11 listener = Streamer()
12 listener.initQueue(output_dir, 3600, 'kw')
13 stream = tweepy.Stream(auth=api.auth, listener=listener)
14 stream.filter(track=keywords)
```

Code Snippet 3.1 Downloading tweets by keyword

There are some caveats to keep in mind. First, there is a limit of 400 keywords on any streamer. Second, searches are case insensitive, i.e. searching for "corona" will also return tweets that include "Corona," "cORona" or any other variation of capitalization. Finally, remember that the streaming API has a hard cap of not allowing the download of more than 1% of the stream at any given point in time. It is not particularly difficult to select a combination of words that exceeds this threshold, at which point the program will begin to throw errors. When setting up a new keyword downloader, keep a careful eye on it to make sure that some of your selected keywords aren't returning more data than you expected.

3.1.2 Downloading Tweets by Language

If your particular research project is centered upon a particular part of the world in which a particular language dominates, one clever trick can be to set up a keyword streamer so that it will download the vast majority of *all* tweets in a given language. The basic principle is to tell the streamer to limit itself to tweets from a certain language, and to then search for keywords that are the stop words for the language in question. Stop words are the short junk words of a language such as pronouns, articles, and prepositions that have little semantic meaning but are ubiquitous in a given language. The term "stop word" originated in the 1950s at the very beginning of the use of computers for sorting text, and indicates that an algorithm should skip over a particular word. In English words such as "the," "he," "she," and "and" are among the most common stop words. One can either look up a stop word list for a given language (there are many such lists available online for every language) or use a built-in list from a Python library in order to simplify your code.

Snippet 3.2 shows this in action in a variant of the keyword streamer we set up in Section 3.1.1, in a file called *snag_lang.py*. Lines 2 through 4 import a library called NLTK (the Natural Language Toolkit, which we will use extensively later in this chapter, and which upon first running will require a download for the language in question). On line 5 we load the stop words for the Swedish language from NLTK, and then on lines 10 through 12 loop through these words in order to create our keywords array. Note that on line 12 we create a new array called languages that will contain a list of the two-letter abbreviations of the languages we want to search. In this case, we set it to "sv," the abbreviation for Swedish. Finally, the only change to the core streamer code is on line 21, telling the filter to only search for this set of keywords in the language in question.

```
1  from Streamer import Streamer
2  import nltk
3  from nltk.corpus import stopwords
4  nltk.download('stopwords')
5  sv_stop = set(stopwords.words('swedish'))
6
7  # Variable definitions
8  output_dir = "queues"
9  keywords = []
10 for s in sv_stop:
11     keywords.append(s)
12 languages = ['sv']
13
```

```
14 auth_handler = OAuthHandler(consumer_key, consumer_secret)
15 auth_handler.set_access_token(access_token, access_token_secret)
16 api = API(auth_handler)
17
18 listener = Streamer()
19 listener.initQueue(output_dir, 1800, 'sv')
20 stream = tweepy.Stream(auth=api.auth, listener=listener)
21 stream.filter(track=keywords, languages=languages)
```

Code Snippet 3.2 Downloading tweets by language

The end result is a streamer that will download all tweets in Swedish that match the stop words of the Swedish language, which will be nearly every tweet in Swedish. This is because stop words are so universal that they appear in virtually any chunk of text in a given language. So long as a particular language represents less than 1% of the total worldwide stream (which is any language other than the ten most common), you should be able to effectively capture all tweets in that language in real time.

Also note that of course you could use the language parameter for any other keyword search in order to limit your keyword matches to tweets in that language.

3.2 Other Content from Tweets

There is a variety of other data available from social media amenable to content analysis besides just the actual text of the tweets. Social media is rich in layers of additional semantic meaning helpfully marked up by the users themselves: namely hashtags (for instance #MeToo) and mentions (for instance, RealDonaldTrump). In addition, social media content is not just text, and often includes links to external content, images, and videos that are also ripe for analysis. This section discusses how to leverage this additional content into a form that can be analyzed.

3.2.1 Hashtags

The use of hashtags by users is helpful for researchers because it represents users self-organizing and labeling content, that is, doing part of our job for us. By using hashtags, users are signaling that their particular tweet is part of a larger conversation with other individuals. The hashtags that a user includes in a tweet have much higher semantic significance than other words because they are chosen explicitly to signal the tweet's purpose.

Worldwide, about 15% of tweets contain hashtags, and 40% of tweets with hashtags contain more than one. The frequency of particular hashtags tends toward a long-tailed distribution, in which a few hashtags are used in hundred of thousands of tweets, while most appear only in a handful. There is enormous variance in how big a daily peak of hashtag usage might be, or even the topical focus of hashtags from entertainment to politics.

In order to integrate hashtags into our infrastructure, we first need to modify the database to accommodate them. Snippet 3.3 shows a bit of Python code to modify any of our existing tweet databases. Since there can be multiple hashtags per tweet, we need a separate table from the tweets table. It is a simple table with just two columns: the hashtag and the unique id of the tweet that it was in. In addition, on the next command, we create a unique index on the combination of the hashtag and tweet id, which will make it efficient for us to search the database table once it is populated.

```
1  # Set up a table for hashtags
2  c.execute("""CREATE TABLE IF NOT EXISTS hashtags (
3               hashtag VARCHAR,
4               tweet_id BIGINT
5          )""")
6  c.execute('''CREATE UNIQUE INDEX IF NOT EXISTS
7               idx_hashtags ON hashtags(tweet_id,hashtag)''')
```

Code Snippet 3.3 Create hashtags table in database

Next, in Snippet 3.4, we create a new method in the tweet class file that we used in Section 2.4.4 that extracts the hashtags from the JSON of a particular tweet. Those are stored in the "entities" section of the JSON that we access on line 3. In line 4 we loop through each of the hashtags in the JSON, and create a hashtag object for each of them and append them to an array. The end result is an array of hashtag objects for each tweet.

```
1      def extractHashtags(s):
2          s.hashtags = []
3          hashtags = s.json['entities'].get('hashtags', [])
4          for h in hashtags:
5              hashtag = Hashtag(s.tweet_id, h)
6              s.hashtags.append(hashtag)
```

Code Snippet 3.4 Method for extracting hashtags from JSON

That hashtag object itself is defined in its own file, shown in Snippet 3.5. Note that it is a very simple object, with just the couple of fields that we set up in the database, and a method for inserting that particular hashtag into the database.

```
 1 class Hashtag:
 2     def __init__(s, tweet_id, h_json):
 3         s.tweet_id = tweet_id
 4         s.hashtag = h_json['text']
 5
 6     def save(s, c):
 7         q = (
 8             s.tweet_id, s.hashtag
 9         )
10         c.execute(
11             """REPLACE INTO hashtags
12             (tweet_id, hashtag)
13             VALUES(?,?)""", q)
```

Code Snippet 3.5 Hashtag class

Finally, Snippet 3.6 shows a modification to our processor program to also insert hashtags into the database. The only changes to our existing processor is to extract the hashtags on line 8, using the function that we just set up, and then looping through and saving each hashtag for each tweet on lines 10–11.

```
 1 # Extract hashtags and write to database
 2 i = 0
 3 conn = sqlite3.connect(outputDB)
 4 c = conn.cursor()
 5 for tweet in tweets:
 6     i += 1
 7     log(str(i) + " of " + str(len(tweets)))
 8     tweet.extractHashtags()
 9     tweet.insert(c)
10     for hashtag in tweet.hashtags:
11         hashtag.save(c)
12 conn.commit()
13 conn.close()
```

Code Snippet 3.6 Modification to processor for hashtags

What does this process gain us? By organizing and collating the hashtags into the database, we can easily aggregate and analyze patterns in the hashtags. For example, if our particular database has been collecting all of the tweets using certain keywords or from a certain group of accounts of interest, then it would be valuable to know what the most frequently used hashtags are in our dataset. With this infrastructure, doing so is as easy as running the SQL in Snippet 3.7, either from within a Python script (where one could export the results directly to a CSV file or perform other analysis on them), or directly from inside a SQLite Browser. In this code, we are telling it to count the number of rows that exist for each distinct hashtag (the "group by" clause tells it which column is the one we want to aggregate by), ordered by that count in descending (DESC) order.

```
1  SELECT COUNT(*),hashtag
2  FROM hashtags
3  GROUP BY hashtag
4  ORDER BY COUNT(*) DESC;
```

Code Snippet 3.7 Selecting most common hashtags

3.2.2 Mentions

Mentions function as a way to include other individuals in a conversation as, when someone's handle is mentioned in a tweet, they are notified. When replying to someone else's tweet, Twitter automatically adds their handle so that they are mentioned. Frequently when a conversation between two individuals is occurring via tweets (replying back and forth), a third person will be mentioned at some point in order to bring them into the conversation. One can go down a rabbit hole of terminology in which such an act is called "tagging" (because you tag them), while mentioning someone who is being talked about so that they know about it (against the wishes of those talking) is called "snitch tagging." Talking about someone without mentioning them is referred to as "subtweeting." The language of the Internet is in constant flux, so while all of the code in this book will remain valid for some time, this paragraph is likely to be the first part of it to become laughably outdated.

Mentions are ubiquitous on Twitter, if only because any reply or retweet will mention the poster of the original tweet. Even looking only at nonretweets, 57% of tweets have at least one mention, providing at least superficial evidence of the *social* element of social media. In this section, we will set up a system for extracting the mentions from our collected tweets and storing them in a database. This process will be very similar to the process of handling hashtags as both items behave similarly in practice.

Mentions are stored in the JSON of individual tweets almost identically to hashtags, and we would like to store them in a very similar way. Snippet 3.8 modifies our database to include a table called "mentions" that has three fields: the mentioned handle (or screen name), the unique id of the user, and the unique id of the tweet. It additionally adds an index for efficient searching of this table.

```
1  # Set up a table for mentions
2  c.execute("""CREATE TABLE IF NOT EXISTS mentions (
3              user_id BIGINT,
4              screen_name VARCHAR,
5              tweet_id BIGINT
6          )""")
7  c.execute('''CREATE UNIQUE INDEX IF NOT EXISTS
8              idx_mentions ON mentions(tweet_id,user_id)''')
```

Code Snippet 3.8 Create mentions table in database

Snippet 3.9 is a method we add to our Tweet object that contains the logic for extracting the mentions from the JSON of a particular tweet. Note that it basically functions the same as hashtag extraction, looping through the "user_mentions" section of the entities object, but also checks to see if the mentioned user is the same as the user who posted the current tweet in line 6. If so, it does not add that mention to the array. The reason for this is that in a long chain of replies and retweets, often the current user's handle is mentioned. However, these self-mentions are just white noise in the sense that we already know that user is part of the conversation since they are the one who posted it, and thus we can exclude it for the sake of parsimony.

```
1      def extractMentions(s):
2          s.mentions = []
3          mentions = s.json['entities'].get('user_mentions', [])
4          for m in mentions:
5              mention = Mention(s.tweet_id, m)
6              if mention.user_id != s.user_id:
7                  s.mentions.append(mention)
```

Code Snippet 3.9 Method for extracting mentions from JSON

Next, Snippet 3.10 defines our mention object, which includes a method for saving the mention to the database that we just set up.

```
1  class Mention:
2      def __init__(s, tweet_id, m_json):
3          s.tweet_id = tweet_id
4          s.user_id = m_json['id']
5          s.screen_name = m_json['screen_name']
6
7      def save(s, c):
8          q = (
9              s.tweet_id, s.user_id, s.screen_name
10             )
11             c.execute(
```

```
12          """REPLACE INTO mentions
13          (tweet_id, user_id, screen_name)
14          VALUES(?,?,?)""", q)
```

Code Snippet 3.10 Mention class

Finally, Snippet 3.11 shows a modification to our processor for extracting these mentions and adding them to the database. Note that if we wanted both hashtags and mentions, we could simply have a single processor that combined the *extractHashtags* and *extractMentions* functionality in one loop.

```
 1  # Extract mentions and write to database
 2  i = 0
 3  conn = sqlite3.connect(outputDB)
 4  c = conn.cursor()
 5  for tweet in tweets:
 6      i += 1
 7      log(str(i) + " of " + str(len(tweets)))
 8      tweet.extractMentions()
 9      tweet.insert(c)
10      for mention in tweet.mentions:
11          mention.save(c)
12  conn.commit()
13  conn.close()
```

Code Snippet 3.11 Modification to processor for mentions

3.2.3 Links and Their Content

Links to external content (for instance, posting a link to a news article) are a very common way for users to communicate additional content beyond the actual text that they post, with approximately 5% of tweets containing at least one URL. This subsection shows how to extract those URLs from the tweet application programming interface (API) object, store them in a database, and even download copies of those external webpages for content analysis.

First, in Snippet 3.12, we create the database table for tracking these URLs. Note that we not only track the unique *tweet_id* and the *URL* itself, but have additional fields for *file* (which will contain the name of the local file when we download this page) and *downloaded* (which will be either True or False depending on whether we have downloaded the URL yet). We also create an index on the combination of the *tweet_id* and *URL* for quick searching.

```
1  c.execute("""CREATE TABLE IF NOT EXISTS urls (
2                  tweet_id BIGINT,
3                  url VARCHAR,
4                  file VARCHAR,
5                  downloaded BOOLEAN
6              )""")
7  c.execute('''CREATE UNIQUE INDEX IF NOT EXISTS
8                  idx_url ON urls(tweet_id,url)''')
```

Code Snippet 3.12 Create URLs table in database

In order to populate this table, we will simply modify our existing processing program (*process_all.py*) that we have used several times now in order to extract the URLs from the JSON files as we go, as shown in Snippet 3.13. While the rest of the program remains the same, we add some code to the loop at the end that inserts each tweet into the database. Line 10 calls the new method *extractURLs()* (which we will look at in detail in a moment) on each tweet, which pulls the URLs out of the JSON for each tweet and stores them in an array called *tweet.urls*. Lines 12 through 15 loop through the URLs, insert the record into the database (with *url.insert*), and in addition download the linked HTML page (with *url.download*). In the latter command we specify the directory that we want to store these files in, and also assign an integer to each URL per tweet, that is, since each tweet can have multiple links, this is simply indicating the first, second, third, etc. for labeling purposes.

```
1  # Write those tweets and URLs to the database
2  outputDir = "files/"
3  i = 0
4  conn = sqlite3.connect(outputDB)
5  c = conn.cursor()
6  for tweet in tweets:
7      i += 1
8      log(str(i) + " of " + str(len(tweets)))
9      tweet.insert(c)
10     tweet.extractURLs()
11     num = 0
12     for url in tweet.urls:
13         num += 1
14         url.insert(c)
15         url.download(c, outputDir, num)
16 conn.commit()
17 conn.close()
```

Code Snippet 3.13 Process JSON files to extract URLs for each tweet

Now let's examine how these new commands are working underneath the hood. First, in Snippet 3.14 we can see the *extractURLs* method that we added to the tweet object. In line 2, it sets up an empty array, and then checks to see on the next line if there are any URLs defined in the appropriate place in this tweet's JSON. If so, it loops through and processes them with our second new method *processURL*. However, because often users reply to an existing tweet that contains a URL, we also want to get any URLs referenced in the quoted status if it exists, which is what is accomplished in lines 7 through 9. The reason for this is that a large number of tweets are *nothing* but an URL with no additional commentary, for example when a user copy and pastes the URL of a news article they enjoyed, and tweet that by itself. When this is done by users with large numbers of followers, many people will reply to that initial tweet and add their own commentary. However, that commentary is almost entirely missing the appropriate context unless the URL of the quoted status URL is also included.

```
1    def extractURLs(s):
2        s.urls = []
3        if 'urls' in s.json['entities']:
4            for u in s.json['entities']['urls']:
5                s.processURL(u)
6        # next grab any URLs in the quoted status
7        if 'quoted_status' in s.json:
8            for u in s.json['quoted_status']['entities']['urls']:
9                s.processURL(u)
10
11   def processURL(s, raw_url):
12       tweet_id = s.tweet_id
13       url = raw_url['expanded_url']
14       my_url = URL(tweet_id, url)
15       # only grab external URLs
16       if not (url.startswith('https://twitter.com/')):
17           s.urls.append(my_url)
```

Code Snippet 3.14 Methods for processing URLs

The method *processURL* is displayed on lines 11 through 17 of Snippet 3.14. While strictly speaking, the URL is extracted directly from the *entities* object, there is some additional processing that needs to be done to make it useful. First, in line 13, we pull out what is called the "expanded_url" from the JSON URL object. This is to ensure that we have the full original URL that the user copy and pasted rather than any shortened version of it used as an internal reference by the Twitter API. Second, on lines 16 and 17 note that we only add this URL to our list if it does *not* start with "https://twitter.com." When tweets are replied to, the URL of that original tweet is in the text of the new tweet and so it ends up in the array of URLs in JSON. However, everything about that tweet is also stored in the quoted status object, so we are already extracting that text elsewhere in

Chapter 2. As such, since this particular application is concerned with *external* links, we screen out those internal Twitter links.

Finally, on line 14 we create an URL object in Python. This is similar to the way that we defined a tweet object in Chapter 2. The purpose of this is to store all of the methods or functions that have to do with individual URLs in one centralized location. This class's source code is displayed in Snippet 3.15. Lines 7 through 14 are simply inserting this URL into the database (and is what was called with *url.insert* in the processing program), while lines 16 through 30 are downloading the URL, saving it to a local file, and updating the database accordingly. Note that line 17 defines the name of the local file as simply being the unique id of the tweet followed by the corresponding number of the URL. For instance if tweet id 123456789 contained two links, this would download them to 123456789_1.html and 123456789_2.html, respectively. We wrap the actual download command on line 19 in a try/except statement so that if a URL has been taken down or is inaccessible the code just marks the URL as *not* downloaded and moves on.

```
 1  class URL:
 2      def __init__(s, tweet_id, url):
 3          s.tweet_id = tweet_id
 4          s.url = url
 5          s.downloaded = False
 6
 7      def insert(s, c):
 8          q = (
 9              s.tweet_id, s.url
10          )
11          c.execute(
12              """REPLACE INTO urls
13                  (tweet_id, url)
14                  VALUES(?,?)""", q)
15
16      def download(s, c, outputDir, num):
17          s.file = outputDir + str(s.tweet_id) + '_' + str(num) + '.html'
18          try:
19              wget.download(s.url, out=s.file)
20              s.downloaded = True
21          except:
22              s.downloaded = False
23          q = (
24              s.file, s.downloaded,
25              s.url, s.tweet_id
26          )
27          c.execute(
28              """UPDATE urls SET
29                  file=?, downloaded=?
30                  WHERE url=? AND tweet_id=?""", q)
```

Code Snippet 3.15 URL class

Upon downloading the content of all the URLs, you now have an additional massive body of text that can be used for textual content analysis purposes, using the techniques discussed in Section 3.3.

If you would like to extract the URLs but not actually download the external web pages (which can be a lengthy and very space-consuming process), all you need to do is comment out or delete line 15 of Snippet 3.13. This may be useful for when your project is doing content analysis on the URLs themselves rather than their content. For example, a project might code whether a tweet contains a link to a partisan news source (such as Breitbart or Infowars) simply by examining the URL for the presence of those domain names.

3.2.4 Extracting and Downloading Images

Images are a rich part of social media data, with people increasingly communicating not just via text, but via the posting of imagery. Some 26% of tweets contain at least one image; however, one should note that this is dominated by retweets, with only 13% of nonretweets containing an image. Often, these images are not in parallel with the text (the way that images on the side of a newspaper article might add supplementary visuals) but operate directly with the text as part of the dialog. This section walks through how to programmatically extract images from tweet objects and download them en masse for analysis. First, we set up our database tables in Snippet 3.16. Note that this is very similar to the URL set up from Section 3.2.3, with fields for the URL of the image online, the name of the local file we will save it to, and a boolean *downloaded* flag to indicate whether we were able to download it.

```
1  c.execute("""CREATE TABLE IF NOT EXISTS images (
2               file VARCHAR,
3               tweet_id BIGINT,
4               url VARCHAR,
5               checksum VARCHAR,
6               downloaded BOOLEAN
7           )""")
8  c.execute('''CREATE UNIQUE INDEX IF NOT EXISTS
9               idx_file ON images(file)''')
```

Code Snippet 3.16 Setting up database for image downloading

In addition there is a new field called *checksum*. A checksum is a way to essentially take a fingerprint of a particular file. While the mathematics of the process are beyond the scope of this book, suffice to say that a checksum is a long alphanumeric string generated by looking at the bytes of any file. Any two identical files will have the exact same checksum, which makes it a popular way to check to see if a copied file has been digitally copied correctly. While it is technically possible for two different files to have the same checksum, it is not particularly likely. As such, what we can use the checksum for is in identifying *distinct* images in our database even if they have entirely different names and URLs. This is particularly common with images that go viral on social media, where the same image has been copied around the web.

In Snippet 3.17, we show the modification of our JSON processor to extracting and downloading the images present in each tweet in our dataset. We specify in line 2 to save those images to a subdirectory called "images," extract the images from each tweet's JSON with the function called on line 9 (*extract Images*, which creates an array of images for each tweet). We then loop through the images for each tweet on lines 11 through 13 and insert records into the database (*image.insert*) and download the image files themselves (*image.download*). Just as with the URL downloader in Section 3.2.3, if you don't want to immediately download the image files but still extract their info from the JSON, just comment out or delete line 13.

```
1   # Write those tweets to a database file and download images
2   outputDir = "images/"
3   i = 0
4   conn = sqlite3.connect(outputDB)
5   c = conn.cursor()
6   for tweet in tweets:
7       i += 1
8       log(str(i) + " of " + str(len(tweets)))
9       tweet.extractImages(outputDir)
10      tweet.insert(c)
11      for image in tweet.images:
12          image.insert(c)
13          image.download(c)
14  conn.commit()
15  conn.close()
```

Code Snippet 3.17 Modification to processor for images

The image extraction method called above (*extractImages*) can be seen in its entirety in Snippet 3.18. Images can appear in three different places in the JSON of a tweet: associated with the tweet itself, with a tweet that's being quoted, or with a tweet that's being retweeted.

Note that lines 4 through 22 are simply repeating the same logic three times (once for each of those locations) with some small tweaks for each. The basic logic is to access the "media" array for each location in the JSON, and then pass each item from that array to the *procImage* method defined on lines 24 through 31. That method extracts the URL of the image (line 26), figures out the type of image (i.e. JPG, PNG, etc.; line 27), and generates a unique local file name for the image to be downloaded to (lines 28–29). Finally, it creates a new instance of the Image class and appends it to the array of images for this tweet.

If your particular project's logic should not include the images from retweets or quoted statuses, feel free to comment out the sections of code on lines 9 through 22 as appropriate (or create your own versions of the methods). Remember though that quoted and retweeted statuses are often used by the user seamlessly with their own added text, so removing that content entirely may remove the context of the original text and content.

```
1    def extractImages(s, outputDir):
2        s.images = []
3        i = 0
4        if 'extended_entities' in s.json:
5            media = s.json['extended_entities'].get('media', [])
6            for m in media:
7                i += 1
8                s.procImage(m, i, outputDir)
9        if 'quoted_status' in s.json:
10           q_json = s.json['quoted_status']
11           if 'extended_entities' in q_json:
12               media = q_json['extended_entities'].get('media', [])
13               for m in media:
14                   i += 1
15                   s.procImage(m, i, outputDir)
16       if 'retweeted_status' in s.json:
17           q_json = s.json['retweeted_status']
18           if 'extended_entities' in q_json:
19               media = q_json['extended_entities'].get('media', [])
20               for m in media:
21                   i += 1
22                   s.procImage(m, i, outputDir)
23
24   def procImage(s, img, num, outputDir):
25       tweet_id = s.tweet_id
26       url = img['media_url']
27       file_type = getFileExtension(url)
28       file_name = str(tweet_id) + '_' + str(num) + file_type
29       output_file = outputDir + file_name
30       image = Image(tweet_id, output_file, url)
31       s.images.append(image)
```

Code Snippet 3.18 Methods for extracting images from JSON

The Image class itself is shown in Snippet 3.19, with an insert method and a download method. The former simply adds a record to our database for this particular image, with default values of None and False for the checksum and downloaded flag, respectively. The download method is nearly identical to the download function for URLs, with the addition of line 21, which calculates the alphanumeric checksum for this particular file once downloaded.

```
 1 class Image:
 2     def __init__(s, tweet_id, file, url):
 3         s.tweet_id = tweet_id
 4         s.file = file
 5         s.url = url
 6         s.checksum = None
 7         s.downloaded = False
 8
 9     def insert(s, c):
10         q = (
11             s.tweet_id, s.file, s.url, s.downloaded
12         )
13         c.execute(
14             """REPLACE INTO images
15             (tweet_id, file, url, downloaded)
16             VALUES(?,?,?,?)""", q)
17
18     def download(s, c):
19         try:
20             wget.download(s.url, out=s.file)
21             s.checksum = getMD5(s.file)
22             s.downloaded = True
23         except:
24             s.checksum = None
25             s.downloaded = False
26
27         q = (
28             s.checksum, s.downloaded, s.tweet_id
29         )
30         c.execute(
31             """UPDATE images SET
32             checksum=?,downloaded=?
33             WHERE file=?""", q)
```

Code Snippet 3.19 The image object

Alternately, since processing JSON files is very fast, but downloading thousands of images is very slow, we might want to design the system to work such that it extracts the image data from the JSON, but holds off on the downloads until later. Delaying on the second step is a simple matter of commenting out the download step as noted above, but we also need to build a separate program for doing the downloading separately. This is relatively easy to do because we can reuse most of the methods and tools from the rest of this section. Snippet 3.20 shows a new method we added to the BasicTweet class. It takes as an input a database connection (*c*) and then connects to the database and grabs all of the image data associated with the current tweet and saves them in the tweet's image array.

```
1    def getImages(s, c):
2        s.images = []
3        for r in c.execute("""SELECT tweet_id, file, url, checksum,
4                              downloaded FROM tweets
5                              WHERE tweet_id="""+str(s.tweet_id)):
6            image = Image(r[0], r[1], r[2])
7            image.checksum = r[3]
8            image.downloaded = r[4]
```

Code Snippet 3.20 Grabbing images from the database

Snippet 3.21 shows the core code of *snag_images.py,* which simply connects to our database, grabs all the tweets from it, and loops through each of them individually. Line 5 calls the *get_images* method we just wrote above, while for each image, line 7 downloads the image using the method we wrote earlier in this section. In this way, we can separate the lengthy downloading process from the efficient JSON processing.

```
1   conn = sqlite3.connect(outputDB)
2   c = conn.cursor()
3   for r in c.execute('SELECT id,text FROM tweets'):
4       tweet = BasicTweet(r[0], r[1])
5       tweet.getImages(c)
6       for image in tweet.images:
7           image.download(c)
8   conn.commit()
9   conn.close()
```

Code Snippet 3.21 Saving images to the local file system

For use as data, there are two different routes for using images from social media. The first is to develop a research design around handcoding, i.e. individually examining and evaluating images. This can be fundamentally qualitative, for instance, developing an ethnography of images posted to Twitter accounts by congressional candidates, or some other particular subset of tweets and images that have substantive interest for your project. It can also be quantitative in nature, by developing a rubric that focuses on identifying and classifying attributes of the images for purposes of aggregation and analysis on a statistical level. For instance, creating a spreadsheet of the images from a set of tweets, having human coders mark whether each image contains a substantively important feature, and then aggregating that into a variable.

In addition, work can be done on the very cutting edge using computerized analysis of images. These techniques involve the use of neural nets (which we talk about in Section 3.3.4 for use with text) in order to automatically classify elements of images. A wide variety of applications exist, from identifying whether a particular image contains a person (or even how many people), whether the photo was taken at night or day, or even extensive pretrained libraries that can identify specific classes of objects present in the image (animals, guns, flags, food, etc.). This approach has the advantage of allowing the analysis of enormous quantities of images with little human intervention, but is technically far more challenging to implement. While these techniques are beyond the scope of this book, interested researchers can consult some of the excellent articles published using these methods (Anastasopoulos et al., 2016, 2017; Joo and Steinert-Threlkeld, 2018; Rudinac, Gornishka, and Worring, 2017; Torres and Cantú, 2022; Won, Steinert-Threlkeld, and Joo, 2017; Xi et al., 2020).

3.2.5 Extracting and Downloading Videos

In this section we build the code for mass downloading any video displayed in the tweets. As with images, tweets with attached videos are dominated by retweets. Some 8% of tweets have attached videos, but three-fourths of these are retweets, reflecting that videos tend to be sourced originally from larger more institutional accounts and are then passed around by others. One caveat to keep in mind is that on Twitter, videos also include any animated GIFs attached to a tweet.

The process of extracting and downloading videos is very similar to that of images, and in fact is a bit simpler in a certain respect since there can be at most one video per tweet. Snippet 3.22 shows the modification of the database to include a videos table. Note that it includes three additional fields that are available in the JSON for videos and might be useful: *title* (which could be used for text analysis or identification), *duration* (which is the length of the video in milliseconds), and *type* (either "video" or "animated_gif").

```
1  c.execute("""CREATE TABLE IF NOT EXISTS videos (
2              file VARCHAR,
3              tweet_id BIGINT,
4              url VARCHAR,
5              duration INT,
6              title VARCHAR,
7              type VARCHAR,
8              checksum VARCHAR
9          )""")
10 c.execute('''CREATE UNIQUE INDEX IF NOT EXISTS
11              idx_file ON videos(file)''')
```

Code Snippet 3.22 Setting up database for video downloading

Snippet 3.23 shows the methods *extractVideo* and *procVideo* that have been added to the Tweet object. Similar to the two methods defined for images in Section 3.2.4, the former pulls out the video information from the different locations in the JSON where it can exist, while the latter extracts the specific fields for each video and saves them to a Video object. Note that there are a few bits of logic accommodating the particulars of videos. First, an if statement on line 13 breaks the logic into two parts, treating normal videos and animated GIFs separately. Second, lines 22 through 24 check to see if the video has a defined bit rate, which excludes videos that snuck into the JSON object but were never able to resolve to a working video.

```
1   def extractVideo(s, outputDir):
2       s.video = None
3       s.procVideo(s.json, outputDir)
4       if s.video is None and 'quoted_status' in s.json:
5           s.procVideo(s.json['quoted_status'], outputDir)
6       if s.video is None and 'retweeted_status' in s.json:
7           s.procVideo(s.json['retweeted_status'], outputDir)
8
9   def procVideo(s, tweet_json, outputDir):
10      if 'extended_entities' in tweet_json:
11          media = tweet_json['extended_entities'].get('media', [])
12          vid_type = media[0]['type']
13          if vid_type == "video":
14              title = None
15              if 'title' in media[0]['additional_media_info']:
16                  title = media[0]['additional_media_info']['title']
17              duration = None
18              if 'duration_millis' in media[0]['video_info']:
19                  duration = media[0]['video_info']['duration_millis']
20              url = ''
21              for v in media[0]['video_info']['variants']:
22                  if 'bitrate' in v:
23                      if v['bitrate'] > 0:
24                          url = v['url']
25              if url != '':
26                  file_name = str(s.tweet_id) + '.mp4'
27                  file = outputDir + file_name
28                  s.video = Video(s.tweet_id, file, url, title, duration,
            vid_type)
29          elif vid_type == "animated_gif":
30              title = None
31              duration = None
32              url = media[0]['video_info']['variants'][0]['url']
33              file_name = str(s.tweet_id) + '.gif'
34              file = outputDir + file_name
35              s.video = Video(s.tweet_id, file, url, title, duration,
            vid_type)
```

Code Snippet 3.23 Methods for extracting videos from JSON

The Video class is defined in Snippet 3.24 and is nearly identical to the image one in Section 3.2.4, with only the additional fields for videos added.

```
1  import sys
2  import wget
3  # including the SMaSSD support files
4  sys.path.append("..")
5  from smassd_functions import *
6
7  class Video:
8      def __init__(s, tweet_id, file, url, title, duration, type):
9          s.tweet_id = tweet_id
10         s.file = file
11         s.url = url
12         s.title = title
13         s.duration = duration
14         s.type = type
15
16     def download(s, c):
17         wget.download(s.url, out=s.file)
18         q = (
19             s.tweet_id, s.file, s.url,
20             s.title, s.duration
21         )
22         c.execute(
23             """REPLACE INTO videos
24             (tweet_id, file, url, title, duration, type)
25             VALUES(?,?,?,?,?,?)""", q)
26
27     def checksum(s, c):
28         s.checksum = getMD5(s.file)
29         if s.checksum is not None:
30             q = (s.checksum, s.file)
31             c.execute("""UPDATE videos
32                 SET checksum=?
33                 WHERE file=?""", q)
```

Code Snippet 3.24 The video object

Finally, Snippet 3.25 shows how to modify the processor to extract videos and download them. Once again, line 11 can be commented out if you want to extract the video information from the JSON but not actually download the files. Note that you could easily add your own code here to specify only to download certain videos. For instance, selecting only the videos from tweets that contain certain hashtags, or limiting videos to only those longer than a certain length.

```
1  # Write those tweets to a database file and download the video
2  i = 0
3  conn = sqlite3.connect(outputDB)
4  c = conn.cursor()
```

```
 5  for tweet in tweets:
 6      i += 1
 7      log(str(i) + " of " + str(len(tweets)))
 8      tweet.extractVideo(outputDir)
 9      tweet.insert(c)
10      if tweet.video is not None:
11          tweet.video.download(c)
12  conn.commit()
13  conn.close()
```

Code Snippet 3.25 Modification to processor for video

3.3 Computer Content Analysis of Text

Computer content analysis is the use of computerized algorithms and statistical methods to identify patterns in text. It is especially useful for social media data because we often have more text available than ever could be handcoded. There is a burgeoning literature on the development of new forms of computer content analysis, so this section seeks to highlight the most important tools, each of which is useful for slightly different research designs. Each of these works on the same basic principle: the text of each tweet is broken into an array of the words it contains, an algorithm is run on those word arrays, and the output is a value for each tweet.

3.3.1 Tools for Text

In this section we will set up some tools for use in the rest of the chapter. First, in Snippet 3.26 we modify our database to have three additional fields in the tweets table. These fields correspond to the next three sections of this chapter: polarity (the output of the sentiment analysis algorithm), topic (the output of the topic identification algorithm), and neuralnet (the output of the neural net algorithm).

```
 1  # Variable definitions
 2  tweetDB = "data/tweets.db"
 3
 4  # Set up database structure
 5  conn = sqlite3.connect(tweetDB)
 6  c = conn.cursor()
 7
 8  # Set up a table for tweets
 9  c.execute('ALTER TABLE tweets ADD polarity INT')
10  c.execute('ALTER TABLE tweets ADD topic INT')
```

```
11  c.execute('ALTER TABLE tweets ADD neuralnet INT')
12
13  conn.commit()
14  conn.close()
```

Code Snippet 3.26 Modifying database for content analysis

Next we have created a new class called *TextTweet* in order to handle the content analysis. Its first few lines and constructor are shown in Snippet 3.27. Note that we have set up a very bare-bones set of variables for this class in contrast to previous Tweet objects, with just the unique id, the text of the tweet, the three content analysis outputs, and an array called *words*. In addition, we include two imports in the first couple of lines from the NLTK Python library. This library contains a large variety of tools that are helpful for doing any programming with the processing of text.

```
1  from nltk.tokenize import TweetTokenizer
2  from nltk.stem import WordNetLemmatizer
3
4  class TextTweet:
5      def __init__(s, id, text):
6          s.id = id
7          s.text = text
8          s.polarity = None
9          s.topic = None
10         s.neuralnet = None
11         s.words = []
```

Code Snippet 3.27 Tweet object and methods for text analysis

Snippet 3.28 shows a set of three methods we can use to set up the array of words from each tweet for processing. The first method *tokenize* uses functionality from the NLTK library to create our words array. It contains special logic for tweets in particular, retaining elements of the text like "#" and "@" that are relevant in social media analysis, and ensuring that URLs are maintained consistently rather than broken up into different "words." Line 5 and line 14 have methods for stemming and lemmatization, which are techniques for simplifying words for analysis.

The core concept of both is to simplify words such that word endings don't make semantically identical words count separately. That is, to take off the word ending so that "cat" and "cats" are counted as the same word, in the most trivial example. Stemming is a crude process in which a simple set of word endings for a given language are simply chopped off (leaving behind the "stem" of the word, hence the name). Lemmatization is the same concept, but built with much more nuance for each language. For instance, stemming will run into issues with knowing that "run" and "ran" are the same word because the base word is transformed rather than just appended with a different word ending. However, systematically knowing how to transform words is a complex process for every single language, and hence lemmatization is treated as a separate method applied to text.

In the methods we have defined here, stemming works for nearly every common language, simply by passing a different language's stemmer object to the method; however, the lemmatize function *only* works for English. Different languages would require individual custom libraries installed and the code rewritten to accommodate them.

```
1    def tokenize(s):
2        tokenizer = TweetTokenizer(preserve_case=False)
3        s.words = tokenizer.tokenize(s.text)
4
5    def stemWords(s, stemmer):
6        new_words = []
7        for w in s.words:
8            new_word = w
9            if not (w.startswith('#') or w.startswith('@')):
10               new_word = stemmer.stem(w)
11           new_words.append(new_word)
12       s.words = new_words
13
14   def lemmatizeWords(s):
15       # this only works for English
16       wnl = WordNetLemmatizer()
17       new_words = []
18       for w in s.words:
19           new_word = w
20           if not (w.startswith('#') or w.startswith('@')):
21               new_word = wnl.lemmatize(w)
22           new_words.append(new_word)
23       s.words = new_words
```

Code Snippet 3.28 Tweet object and methods for text analysis

For both methods, they take the existing array of words from a given tweet, loop over it, apply either stemming or lemmatization to each word, and replace the words array with a newly processed one. In addition, note that on lines 9 and 20, the algorithms specifically skip over any words that start with "#" or "@." This is because we don't want mentions and hashtags to go through this process because their semantic meaning is tied to their precise spelling.

Next, in Snippet 3.29 we define a set of several "remove" methods that function to winnow down the word array for each tweet based on some logic.

The first three, *removeMentions*, *removeHashtags*, and *removeURLs* all function almost identically. They each remove words from the list that start with a certain sequence of characters, allowing us to remove all hashtags, mentions, or URLs from the word arrays. These mostly serve to remove noise if we know it exists. For instance, if we are looking at a sample of tweets from a certain language, the mentions might add a lot of distinct words to our data with no semantic benefit. On the other hand, if we are looking specifically at tweets about a very narrow topic within a community that has a few accounts frequently mentioned, those mentions might be extremely semantically rich. Figuring out how to winnow down word lists for a given research project may require some trial and error work.

```python
1    def removeMentions(s):
2        new_words = []
3        for w in s.words:
4            if not (w.startswith('@')):
5                new_words.append(w)
6        s.words = new_words
7
8    def removeHashtags(s):
9        new_words = []
10       for w in s.words:
11           if not (w.startswith('#')):
12               new_words.append(w)
13       s.words = new_words
14
15   def removeURLs(s):
16       new_words = []
17       for w in s.words:
18           if not (w.startswith('http')):
19               new_words.append(w)
20       s.words = new_words
21
22   def removeStopwords(s, stop_words):
23       new_words = []
24       for w in s.words:
25           if w not in stop_words:
26               new_words.append(w)
27       s.words = new_words
28
29   def removeShortwords(s, min_length):
30       new_words = []
31       for w in s.words:
32           if len(w) >= min_length:
33               new_words.append(w)
34       s.words = new_words
```

Code Snippet 3.29 Tweet object and methods for text analysis

On line 22 the method *removeStopwords* is designed to take in an array of words that you have determined do not matter, and then remove them from the word array of each tweet. As we discussed in Section 3.1.2, there are libraries available with the stop words for any common language (i.e. "the," "he," "she," "and," etc. in English) that have no semantic value and can simply be dropped from any analysis. This helps simplify the work of our algorithms. Since this function takes as an input an array of words to remove, it can be used with multiple languages as well. For instance, if you have a collection of tweets from a bilingual population, written interchangeably in Spanish and English, one might call this function twice, passing it both an English and Spanish stop word list.

In addition, there are words that may need to be removed because of the research design itself. Most commonly this has to do with a selection effect. That is, if you selected the tweets on the basis of including a certain set of words, depending on the analysis, you may want to remove that set of words from the tweets before doing automated analysis. For example, if we downloaded all tweets that use the hashtags "#republican" and "#democrat" and wanted to use automated topic identification to sort tweets into two main topics, the output would almost certainly simply sort tweets using each of those hashtags into two bins, regardless of the other words present. This is because those two hashtags would rarely overlap, and therefore would statistically provide perfect separation into two bins. Depending on the research design, this may be exactly what is intended, or may render the results meaningless.

Finally, *removeShortwords* is a helper function for removing very short words, which are often semantically meaningless, even if not on a stop word list. The method simply takes in an integer minimum length, and removes all words from the array that are shorter than that number of characters.

3.3.2 Sentiment Analysis

Sentiment analysis is the process of evaluating text for affective qualities such as emotional content. One of the simplest methods of sentiment analysis is evaluating polarity, which is the net positive or negative sentiment of the text. While problematic for long texts that often contain a multitude of complex emotion, the shortness of social media posts lends itself well to this technique. Polarity at its most basic level can be implemented with a dictionary that assigns a positive, negative, or neutral value to a set of words, and the total value of a given text is calculated by summing the polarities of its constituent words. Snippet 3.30 implements a basic polarity sentiment analysis.

```
 1  from polyglot.downloader import downloader
 2  from polyglot.text import Text
 3
 4  # Variable definitions
 5  tweetsDB = "data/tweets.db"
 6
 7  conn = sqlite3.connect(tweetsDB)
 8  c = conn.cursor()
 9  for r in c.execute('SELECT id,text FROM tweets'):
10      polarity = 0
11      text = Text(r[1])
12      text.language = 'en'
13      for w in text.words:
14          polarity += w.polarity
15      q = (int(polarity), r[0])
16      c.execute("UPDATE tweets SET polarity=? WHERE id=?", q)
17  conn.commit()
18  conn.close()
```

Code Snippet 3.30 Measuring positive/negative polarity of text

On lines 1 and 2 we import a new library called *polyglot* that contains polarity dictionaries for 136 languages. Then we connect to one of our databases and loop through the texts of all the tweets. On line 10 we set the initial polarity of each tweet to zero (that is, neutral) and then load the text of the tweet into objects from the polyglot library. Note that on line 12 we specify which language we want polyglot to use in calculating polarity. In this case, we have hard coded it to English.

Note that the first time you run this code, it will likely give the following error: "ValueError: This resource is available in the index but not downloaded, yet." This is indicating that the polarity dictionaries for the language in question have not been downloaded on your system. To do so, you just need to open a command line and run "polyglot download sentiment.en," where the "en" at the end is the two-letter language code for the dictionaries you want to download. Line 13 loops through the individual words in the text of the tweet and then adds the polarity of that word to the total polarity of the tweet in line 14. Finally, lines 15 and 16 save the tweet's polarity to our database.

One could also implement a completely cross-linguistic polarity analysis here by simply downloading *all* the languages supported by polyglot, and then setting the language of each tweet to the detected language from the tweet object. There are a couple of caveats here. First, different languages will vary in their typical number of words, and the amount of inherent positive or negative speech in the language (whether inherent to the language, or simply the dictionaries for that language). That is, a +4 polarity tweet in English may not be comparably equivalent to a +4 polarity tweet in French. Second, and more mundanely, recall that some of the language codes reported by Twitter do not match the current standards for languages codes, as we discussed in Section 2.3.4 in Chapter 2, so you may need to implement work-arounds for those few.

More advanced sentiment analysis methods are available, although the general rule of thumb is that the more nuanced and sophisticated a method is, the less languages it will be available for since sentiment is inherently language specific. The Stanford CoreNLP library (built in Java) has an extraordinarily sophisticated sentiment analysis infrastructure that is built upon understanding and diagramming the grammar of words and sentences. However, its most advanced tools are only functional for English. In using it for polarity calculations for English it yields very similar results to the polyglot library. For example, in calculating the polarity of all tweets by members of Congress during a session of Congress (about a million tweets total), the estimated polarities using the polyglot and Stanford libraries have a correlation of about 0.9.

One particularly useful advanced method is the identification of emotion in text rather than simply calculating polarity. For example, work by Colnerič and Demsar built upon classic models of emotional categories from psychology in order to train a neural network to recognize and classify dominant emotion (such as anger, joy, sadness, etc.) present in individual English-language tweets (Colnerič and Demsar, 2020). Their emotion identifier is available as a Python library at https://github.com/nikicc/twitter-emotion-recognition.

This more advanced work can be very useful in contexts where we want to tease out specific expressions of emotion as being substantively relevant. For example, Mechkova and Wilson's *Norms and Rage* uses the Colnerič and Demsar sentiment analysis tool to identify the level of expressed anger in tweets about politics during the 2018 American midterm elections (Mechkova and Wilson, 2021). This sentiment analysis model is applied to both tweets by candidates for office and tweets from the public that have been tweeted at candidates for Congress. The result is the ability to test old political science theories about the gendered response to expression of emotion by candidates for office, with a new and far more granular set of data than had ever been available before. Additional work has used similar tools for operationalizing negative versus positive sentiment in congressional campaign tweets (Gelman, Wilson, and Petrarca, 2021), negative speech surrounding tweets about vaccines in dozens of languages worldwide (Wilson and Wiysonge, 2020), and variance in the emotion used in partisan appeals by elites (Gelman and Wilson, 2021).

3.3.3 Topic Modeling

Topic modeling is a statistical process by which collections of texts are grouped together based on similar frequencies of word usage. The process is often called *naive* when it applies algorithms that use minimal assumptions about the texts and allow the topics to emerge organically from the text. Functionally, topic modeling takes as an input a set of texts and a defined number of topics, and outputs an estimate of which topic each text belongs to along with a listing of the most statistically significant words in each topic. Because the process is "naive" it does not have any preconceived assumptions about what the topics are or what words should matter to each. This allows a researcher to apply topic modeling to texts and then qualitatively examine the statistically significant words in order to identify the substantive topic with which those words are associated.

Latent Dirichlet allocation (LDA) is the most commonly used such process in the social sciences, and it functions quite well with social media data. In this section we walk through a working example of topic modeling using LDA in Python on tweets, going step by step through the file *lda.py*. This program selects all tweets from one of our databases, pre-processes the texts, implements an LDA topic model, and then saves the identified topic for each tweet back to the database.

```
 1  from TextTweet import TextTweet
 2  import nltk
 3  from nltk.corpus import stopwords
 4  from nltk.stem import SnowballStemmer
 5  import gensim
 6  from gensim import corpora
 7  from gensim import models
 8  import pyLDAvis.gensim
 9
10  nltk.download('wordnet')
11  nltk.download('stopwords')
12
13  language = 'english'
14  en_stop = set(stopwords.words(language))
15  stemmer = SnowballStemmer(language)
16
17  tweetsDB = "data/tweets.db"
18  outputHTML = "output.html"
19  num_topics = 5
```

Code Snippet 3.31 LDA topic modeling: imports and setup

Snippet 3.31 walks through the first lines of the code that set up the required library imports and definition of parameters. There are several new libraries that need to be installed and imported in order to use LDA: NLTK, GenSim (which contains the topic modeling libraries), and pyLDAvis (which provides visualization tools for the output of LDA). Lines 10 through 15 set up the stop words and stemming objects for the English language. Finally, lines 17–19 establish the basic settings for the program, including the database we want to get tweets from, an HTML file we will output visualization to, and the number of topics we want to sort the texts into.[1]

```
1  # Connect to the database and loop through all tweets
2  tweets = []
3  conn = sqlite3.connect(tweetsDB)
4  c = conn.cursor()
5  for r in c.execute('SELECT id,text FROM tweets'):
6      tweet = TextTweet(r[0], r[1])
7      tweet.tokenize()
8      tweet.removeURLs()
9      tweet.removeStopwords(en_stop)
10     tweet.removeMentions()
11     tweet.removeShortwords(3)
12     #tweet.stemWords(stemmer)
13     tweet.lemmatizeWords()
14     tweets.append(tweet)
15 conn.close()
16 documents = [x.words for x in tweets]
```

Code Snippet 3.32 LDA topic modeling: processing tweet text

Next, in Snippet 3.32, we connect to the database and select all of the tweets within it. Note that at this point we could select a specific subset of tweets if so desired. Within the loop, we set up a TextTweet instance for each tweet on line 6, and then utilize a number of the text methods that we defined earlier in the chapter. We tokenize each tweet on line 7 (thus creating an array of the words it contains) and then remove all URLs, stop words, mentions, and short words, before lemmatizing it. Note that we have commented out the stemming method because we can either stem or lemmatize but not both, and thus opt for the more nuanced method since it is available for the language of these tweets (English). Lastly, the LDA methods require as an input an array of word arrays, and so on line 16 we create an array called "documents" in this format. We call it this for consistency since LDA methods tend to refer to the individual units of text as documents.

---

[1] The number of topics is a key assumption here. There is no correct answer or algorithm for producing the optimum number of topics for a given set of texts. There are statistical tools for providing insight into how coherently separated the topics are, but all rely on the same basic approach of running LDA iteratively assuming different numbers of topics and then comparing their results. They are generally most helpful when used in conjunction with a trial and error approach of examining the output of different runs to see if the statistically significant words form coherent topics from the substantive perspective of the research.

```
1  # Construct and run LDA model
2  dictionary = gensim.corpora.Dictionary(documents)
3  dictionary.filter_extremes(no_below=50, no_above=0.5, keep_n=10000)
4  corpus = [dictionary.doc2bow(x) for x in documents]
5  lda_model = gensim.models.ldamodel.LdaModel(
6      corpus=gensim.models.TfidfModel(corpus)[corpus],
7      id2word=dictionary,
8      num_topics=num_topics)
```

Code Snippet 3.33 LDA topic modeling: Construct and running LDA model

We are now ready to actually run the LDA modeling process, which is shown in Snippet 3.33, and having done all of that setup is surprisingly simple in practice. First, it converts our word arrays into a dictionary (a list of *all* distinct words that appear across all of our tweets, along with the number of times each word appears in each tweet) and then on line 3 runs the method "filter_extremes," which serves to winnow down that dictionary. It does so by getting rid of words that appear in too few of the tweets (no_below, i.e. "no words that appear less than this many times") or too many (no_above, which takes a proportion between 0 and 1). Through trial and error, you can adjust these parameters, but a good rule of thumb to start with is that words that appear in less than 1% or more than 50% of your tweets probably are not very helpful in sorting them, because they either singularly determine a topic or are unhelpful noise because they appear in *all* the topics. The additional parameter "keep_n" provides a hard cap on the total number of words in the dictionary. This is mostly useful in making sure that an error elsewhere does not lead to a memory crash, as most sets of text in a language with reasonable limitations will end up having a few thousand distinct words, with a long tail of uncommonly occurring words. Lines 5 through 8 construct the LDA model using the settings and parameters set in the above code.

```
1   # Loop through and save results of model to database
2   threshold = 0.5
3   conn = sqlite3.connect(tweetsDB)
4   c = conn.cursor()
5   for tweet in tweets:
6       bow = dictionary.doc2bow(tweet.words)
7       topics = lda_model.get_document_topics(bow)
8       max_prob = 0
9       for t in topics:
10          if t[1]>max_prob and t[1]>threshold:
11              max_prob = t[1]
12              tweet.topic = t[0]
```

```
13    if tweet.topic is not None:
14        q = (tweet.topic, tweet.id)
15        c.execute("UPDATE tweets SET topic=? WHERE id=?", q)
16 conn.commit()
17 conn.close()
```

Code Snippet 3.34 LDA topic modeling: saving results of LDA model

This may take a little bit of time to run depending on your computer, but the end result is an object that contains for each tweet a probability that it belongs to each topic. Snippet 3.34 shows how we save that information to our database so that when we're done, the "topic" field of our database contains the topic to which each tweet belongs. On line 2, we set the minimum probability we want to accept. This may need to be tuned for particular applications, but note that setting it too high will lead to a great deal of "N/A" results, and setting it too low will lead to a great deal of noise. For example, if the number of topics is set to five and the tweet is so indeterminate that the algorithm has no idea which topic it belongs in, then each topic will have a probability of 0.2. Lines 9 through 12 simply loop through all of the topics for each tweet and identify the one that is both the maximum and greater than the threshold. And finally, lines 13 through 15 save that result to the database for each tweet (provided at least one of the topics met the minimum threshold, otherwise the tweet's topic will remain blank in the database). Because the topics are naively arrived at by the algorithm they are simply labeled as integers: 1 to the maximum number of topics.

```
1 # Printing out topic details
2 for index, topic in lda_model.print_topics(num_topics=-1, num_words=20):
3     print(str(index)+": "+topic)
4
5 # Generating visualization HTML file
6 lda_display = pyLDAvis.gensim.prepare(lda_model,corpus,dictionary)
7 pyLDAvis.save_html(lda_display,outputHTML)
```

Code Snippet 3.35 LDA topic modeling: viewing and visualizing LDA model output

So how do we actually determine what those numbered topics *mean* in substantive terms? Snippet 3.35 provides two tools for us. First, on line 2, it simply prints out the 20 most statistically significant words from each topic. A researcher can use this to determine what sorts of content are being clustered into each topic. Alternatively, you could write additional code to save these lists to their own database tables, or analyze them in further custom ways. Secondly,

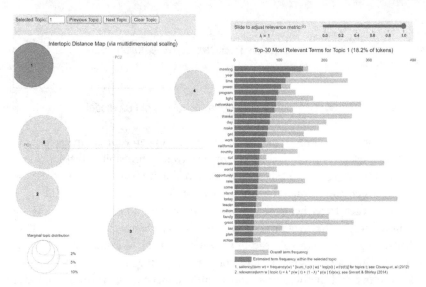

Figure 3.1 Interactive visualization of LDA model output (using pyLDAVis)

on lines 6 and 7, we use the pyLDAVis tool to generate an interactive HTML file that provides visualizations of how statistically separate the topics are, and with a clickable interface for seeing what the statistically significant words are for each topic. This file can be opened in any web browser on your computer, and a screenshot of it in action is seen in Figure 3.1.

This process works well if we have a strong theoretical expectation about the number of topics that are likely in our corpus of texts. In that case, the number of topics defined in the LDA model should usually be that expectation plus one, so that there is a residual topic in addition to the "expected" topics. However, there are additional statistical tools available for assessing the statistically appropriate number of topics for a given body of texts. Each of these essentially iteratively runs an LDA model with different numbers of topics and provides statistical metrics of *coherence* and *perplexity*. Discussion of those metrics is beyond the scope of this introduction, but the code provided can be easily modified to loop through different numbers of topics and then produce those scores for each iteration for further evaluation as to the optimum number of topics for a given set of texts.

In addition, depending on how tightly focused the body of tweets being analyzed is topically, LDA models can sometimes struggle to classify well on the short number of words present in tweets. If this problem emerges, it is often useful to aggregate the tweets together into larger individual units based on the substantive dimensions of the research. For instance, if we are interested in the temporal variance of topics, we might aggregate together all tweets by each user on a monthly basis, so that instead of our unit of analysis being the individual tweet, it is at the user-month level. Or if our research question is focused at classifying the behavior of users, we might aggregate all tweets by each user together. All of the tools presented in this text can be used on aggregated tweets.

3.3.4 Supervised Learning Models

Supervised learning is the process by which we use statistical tools to classify texts based on predefined classification developed by the researcher. This allows a great deal of additional power because it enables us to construct measures based on our substantive research questions. At its simplest, this can be simply a detector of a predefined dictionary of words. For instance, if we wanted to measure the incidence of racist tweets, we could create a dictionary of racist terms and then write a simple program to flag which tweets contained those terms. For concepts for which the *way* they are discussed is well understood and easily delineated, this can be a sufficient approach. However, it can also be vulnerable to selection effects: We only find what we look for.

Supervised models function by having us hand code a fraction of the total texts, building a model based on those texts and our hand coding, and then applying that model across the rest of the texts. The idea is that the computer mimics what hand coders would do if we had the time and resources to actually code the full sets of texts. Once we trust a model, we can then apply it to new texts so long as the new texts are interchangeably comparable with the characteristics of the initial texts. We do need to beware of "concept drift," however, in which over time texts gradually morph in characteristics, since human speech about any topic evolves quickly, adding new terms as events occur, shading the meaning of old terms in newly interpreted ways. So over time a model will become less accurate, but we can judge that process by hand coding samples of newly acquired texts, and testing the model on them to see if it is still reliable, or is slipping in systematic ways. As we see drift, we can either train new models on new texts, or build a new catch-all model trained on both old and new texts. In either case, follow the iterative process of hand coding, testing out-of-sample predictions, and evaluating model performance.

Taking the racist tweet example, we could for instance have collected the tens of millions of tweets in which Americans mention members of Congress, and have substantive research questions revolving around the use of hate speech toward politicians. This is vastly more data than any human could hope to code, and any creation of a dictionary of terms would likely be plagued by missingness due to the ever-evolving use of dog whistling, in which harmless phrasing and terms are used in appropriate context to signal hate. But if we took a random sample of tweets mentioning politicians, hand coded a sample of some few thousand tweets with a dichotomous indicator of whether they were racist or not, that subset of tweets could be used to train a model of racist speech that captures the subtleties of such speech. Note that this process allows for all of the usual techniques of data coding to be employed: appropriate selection of a sample, coding by multiple coders for intercoder reliability testing, cross-validation of results, iterative coding of problematic cases, etc. And the constant evolution of racist speech demonstrates how concept drift necessitates a constant updating and reevaluating of such models over time.

There are a wide variety of supervised learning models, including support-vector machines (SVM) and random forest models. The current state of the art in supervised text classification is the use of neural networks, a form of machine learning that is conceptually modeled on the way that pattern recognition functions in biological brains. Neural network models take as an input a set of features (in text data the input will be an array of word frequencies) and an output (in our example, a dichotomous flag of whether the tweet is racist or not) and assume that there is a connection between each potential combination of input features. Imagine a network in which every word in a language is a node, and there is a line drawn between each word and every other. If two words rarely show up together in a text, the connection between would be very weak. Stop words would have strong connections with almost all other words.

While neural nets are more complex to implement than other supervised learning models, their status as the current cutting edge, in combination with other utilities, makes their mastery worth the while of anyone wanting to leverage computerized supervised learning models in the context of social media data. Because neural nets support multiple "layers" of pretrained models, we can use existing models that have been trained by other scholars in other contexts to enhance the performance of our particular models beyond just the texts we have on hand for training. A common approach is to include as a layer a model pretrained on all Wikipedia articles in the appropriate language in order to give the model a sense of how text generally works in the language in question as opposed to simply relying on the texts of our individual research project. The *HuggingFace.co* repository contains a massive, and growing, selection of models across dozens of languages built along standardized models for layering seamlessly into custom neural net models. For a social scientific example in practice, see Hashemi, Wilson, and Petrarca's *Investigating the Iranian Twittersphere*, which utilizes existing pretrained models of millions of Persian-language news articles to classify the broad topic of tweets in that language, in addition to building different models that classify named entities (proper place names, people, and organizations) mentioned in their Twitter corpus (Hashemi, Wilson, and Petrarca, 2022).

Training texts work by telling the machine how the texts we care about *differ* from usual texts in the language. For example, if two words frequently show up together in the *racist* training texts but not the other texts, the fact that the connection between those two words is strong in our relevant texts but *not* in other texts is important information. Now consider that there is a function that compresses those nodes and connections down to a simpler network, with fewer nodes as the uninformative connections are discarded. These are the *layers* of a neural network, in which each network's output constructs a simpler network iteratively highlighting the connections and interconnections of different words, eventually winnowing down to the desired output of a simple dichotomous flag.

In this section we walk through a very simple neural network that will allow you to implement supervised classification with only small modifications to your particular project's logic. First, we are starting from the assumption that training texts are available. As an example, I have included a set of 5 000 trained tweets from members of Congress in the few weeks leading up to the 2018 midterm elections (*neuralnet_trained.csv*).[2] This file contains three columns: the tweet's unique id, the text of the tweet, and a field called "neuralnet," which is our hand-coded dichotomous variable. In this case, the variable is indicating whether the tweet contains "get out the vote" language, i.e. encouraging people to vote. Note that one could easily code multiple fields and set up a neural net for each of them (in the original project, we hand coded a half dozen fields for each tweet to indicate various additional elements such as partisanship, ideology, etc.). In addition, one can just as easily have multiple values in this field; neural nets do not require it to be dichotomous. For example, one could treat this as a more traditional topic modeling exercise and hand code each tweet as one of a set of topics.

In practice, one would select an appropriately sized random sample from a larger table of tweets in order to generate the CSV file in the first place for hand coders to use in Excel. And once intercoder reliability checks and the synthesis of any disagreements was managed, a CSV file like this could be imported back into your database. Snippet 3.36 shows the creation of a table with just these training tweets. Lines 8–14 create the table, while lines 17–25 show the importation of data from the CSV file. In addition, note that lines 27 and 28 set the value of a field called "training" to one and then set a random sample of 1 in 10 of the imported tweets to zero. The SQL function "RANDOM()" generates a random integer and the "%" operator is modulo division, which means that it returns the remainder of the division. That is, this bit of code divides by 10 and returns the remainder. By checking to see if the remainder is zero, we are effectively grabbing a random sample of 1 in 10 tweets, since 1 in 10 random numbers will be divisible by 10.

---

[2] Thanks to Jeremy Gelman for the use of this training data, and our research assistant Mackenzie Robinson, who each hand coded this full random sample of tweets.

The reason we do this last bit is so that we can use 90% of the hand-coded tweets for training our model (those with training = 1), and reserve 10% of them for an out-of-sample test set (those with training = 0). That is, we will have roughly 500 tweets that we know the correct coding to, that we can apply the model to in order to see how well it does.

```
1  # Variable definitions
2  tweetDB = "data/tweets.db"
3
4  # Set up database structure
5  conn = sqlite3.connect(tweetDB)
6  c = conn.cursor()
7
8  # Set up a table for training tweets
9  c.execute('''CREATE TABLE training_tweets (
10              id BIGINT,
11              text VARCHAR,
12              neuralnet INT,
13              training INT
14          )''')
15
16 # Open CSV file:
17 d = pd.read_csv("neuralnet_trained.csv")
18 for i in range(0,len(d['id'])):
19     q = (int(d['id'][i]),
20             d['text'][i],
21             int(d['neuralnet'][i])
22         )
23     c.execute(
24         """REPLACE INTO training_tweets
25         (id, text, neuralnet) VALUES(?,?,?)""", q)
26
27 c.execute("UPDATE training_tweets SET training=1")
28 c.execute("UPDATE training_tweets SET training=0 WHERE RANDOM()%10=0")
29
30 conn.commit()
31 conn.close()
```

Code Snippet 3.36 Importing training data for neural net

Next we will go through the file *neuralnet_training.py* bit by bit. Snippet 3.37 shows the importation of libraries and some basic setup of objects that the neural net will use. This uses a new library called Keras (which is built upon an additional library called Tensor Flow) that handles the bulk of the neural network analysis for us.

```
 1 ##########################################
 2 from TextTweet import TextTweet
 3 import nltk
 4 from nltk.corpus import stopwords
 5 from keras.preprocessing.text import Tokenizer
 6 from keras.utils import np_utils
 7 from sklearn.preprocessing import LabelEncoder
 8 from keras.models import Sequential
 9 from keras.layers import Dense, Dropout, Activation
10 from sklearn.metrics import confusion_matrix
11 nltk.download('wordnet')
12 nltk.download('stopwords')
13 tokenizer = Tokenizer()
14 encoder = LabelEncoder()
```

Code Snippet 3.37 Neural net training: libraries

Snippet 3.38 shows the initial parameters for our neural network. These are the values that would need modified were you to create your own neural network with different settings. We establish the tweets database we will be using, the set of stop words we want to screen out, and then lines 3 and 4 set up the number of categories in our model. In our case, since we have a dichotomous indicator that takes a value of either 0 or 1, those are the values in our array of labels. Finally, we define the prefix of the output files of our model. Neural nets can be saved to disk for later use, but doing so creates a number of files, so this value is used to prepend the name of each file so all the files of a particular model have predictable names.

```
1 tweetsDB = "data/tweets.db"
2 en_stop = set(stopwords.words('english'))
3 labels = [0, 1]
4 num_categories = len(labels)
5 output_file = "nn"
```

Code Snippet 3.38 Neural net training: setup and parameters

Next we will select the training tweets from the database and put them in a form that is usable by the neural net libraries. Snippet 3.39 begins by setting up four arrays, which correspond to the texts and the output (i.e. "get out the vote" or note) for the training and testing tweets, respectively. In lines 6–22 we select tweets from the database, and then run their text through our special text functions one by one. We then check to see on lines 16–21 whether the particular tweet is for training or testing, and append it to the appropriate arrays. The end result is a list of texts and a list of outputs for training and testing. Lines 24 and 25 generate complete lists of all words that show up in the training texts, while lines 26 and 27 use helper functions to reformat the testing and training texts based on those word lists, so that they are transformed into arrays indicating whether each tweet includes each word that appears in the training texts. For example, if we have a training set of 4 500 tweets that included 2 500 distinct words after all of our preprocessing, this will create an array of 4 500 arrays of 2 500 elements each. Further, if the testing set was an additional 500 tweets, it will be converted into an array of 500 arrays of the same 2 500 elements. Finally, line 28 reformats the training output into a format usable by the neural net software.

```
1  train_text = []
2  train_output = []
3  test_text = []
4  test_output = []
5
6  conn = sqlite3.connect(tweetsDB)
7  c = conn.cursor()
8  for r in c.execute('SELECT id,text,neuralnet,training FROM training_tweets'):
9      tweet = TextTweet(r[0], r[1])
10     tweet.tokenize()
11     tweet.removeURLs()
12     tweet.removeStopwords(en_stop)
13     tweet.removeMentions()
14     tweet.removeShortwords(3)
15     processed_text = ' '.join(tweet.words)
16     if r[3]==0:
17         test_text.append(processed_text)
18         test_output.append(r[2])
19     else:
20         train_text.append(processed_text)
21         train_output.append(r[2])
22 conn.close()
23
24 tokenizer.fit_on_texts(train_text)
25 dictionary = tokenizer.word_index
26 train_text = prep_training(train_text, dictionary, tokenizer)
27 test_text = prep_text(test_text,dictionary,tokenizer)
28 train_output = np_utils.to_categorical(encoder.fit_transform(train_output))
```

Code Snippet 3.39 Neural net training: setting up training and test data

Now we have everything we need to construct a neural net model. Snippet 3.40 demonstrates a minimalist neural network. Lines 1 through 6 set up the layers of the neural network. The details and settings included are beyond the scope of this discussion, but the important components for writing your own code are understanding what needs to be tweaked for different neural nets. On line 2, we define the shape of the input data (i.e. the number of words in the dictionary) and on line 6 we define the shape of the output (i.e. the number of different output values). In both cases, it is calculating those values from our data, but it is important to understand those are determined by your data rather than being part of the model's settings. Lines 8–10 set up the model, while lines 12–17 fit the model to your data (*train_text* and *train_output*).

This is the step that can take a long time to run, varying greatly based on the complexity of your data and the strength of your computer hardware. In practice, the subjectiveness of the trained concept seems to be the driving factor in computation time here. For example, in the project where we hand coded "get out the vote" tweets and "partisanship," both were run on the same texts, and both were dichotomous outputs; however, the partisanship model took nearly 10 times as long to derive. This makes sense: Get out the vote messages will reasonably be a simple concept to capture with a limited set of words like "vote" doing most of the work, while partisanship is a more fluid and nuanced concept. Both neural nets once constructed performed well on out-of-sample tests, although the more subjective concept was a few percentage points less accurate overall.

```
1  model = Sequential()
2  model.add(Dense(512, input_shape=(len(dictionary)+1,), activation='relu'))
3  model.add(Dropout(0.5))
4  model.add(Dense(256, activation='tanh'))
5  model.add(Dropout(0.5))
6  model.add(Dense(num_categories, activation='sigmoid'))
7
8  model.compile(loss='categorical_crossentropy',
9                optimizer='adam',
10               metrics=['accuracy'])
11
12 model.fit(train_text, train_output,
13           batch_size=32,
14           epochs=10,
15           verbose=1,
16           validation_split=0.2,
17           shuffle=True)
```

Code Snippet 3.40 Neural net training: running the neural net model

Now that we have a model, we need to see how well it performs on our out-of-sample testing tweets. Snippet 3.41 creates an array called *predictions* that will store the predicted values of the model that we can compare to the actual hand-coded outputs. Lines 2–5 loop through our test tweets and one by one apply the neural net model to them. Finally, line 6 constructs a confusion matrix and prints it out so we can examine it for false positive and false negative rates.

While accuracy depends a great deal on the complexity of the task, the quality of the training data, and the overall quantity of data that the neural net can work with, high accuracy neural nets are possible. The examples these projects were drawn from both achieved over 90% total accuracy in out-of-sample tests (Gelman and Wilson, 2021; Gelman, Wilson, and Petrarca, 2021). Finally, line 9 saves the neural net to a local file (in a directory called *models*) so that we can later apply this same model to additional tweets without having to redo the entire modeling process.

```
1  predictions = []
2  for t in test_text:
3      raw_pred = model.predict(t)
4      pred = labels[np.argmax(raw_pred)]
5      predictions.append(pred)
6  cm = confusion_matrix(test_output, predictions)
7  pprint.pprint(cm)
8
9  save_model("nn",dictionary,model)
```

Code Snippet 3.41 Neural net training: evaluating and saving the model

Creating a neural net model like this for a project should be an iterative process. A researcher should take the out-of-sample results and examine the false positives and false negatives for any discernible patterns. Additional code can be written to take into account patterns that are human identifiable but aren't being picked up by machine learning. For example, we noted in our work that a large number of partisan tweets that were classified as false negatives had minimal text but included links to highly partisan news sources (such as Breitbart), and so we wrote a simple bit of code that ran after the neural net that automatically classified tweets with such URLs as partisan, thus solving our false negative problem.

In addition, there are often elements external to the text of the tweets that provide information salient to the machine learning. For example, our congressional tweets database can easily be merged with a database of attributes of the politicians themselves (such as gender, race, party membership, or attributes of their congressional district). If appropriate for our analysis, we can inject these attributes as inputs into the neural network by simply adding them as "words" to each tweet as appropriate. For instance, in one congressional campaign project we used neural nets to identify attack tweets, for which mentioning the Twitter handle of one's opponent in the race was a substantively significant signal. But this signal was impossible for the neural net to pick up on because it did not have the context for knowing that a certain mention in a certain set of tweets mattered, but didn't matter in others. So we wrote code that contextually identified the Twitter handle of each handle's opponent, and then flagged whether each tweet contained that mention as appropriate. For the neural net we simply appended the word "opponentmention" to any tweet where that was the case, thus introducing a "word" that the neural net could model along with the others.

One additional trick is to use existing texts as the training data to eliminate the human coding step entirely. This can be useful when we have a certain subset of tweets that can be classified on the basis of some attributes of their users. For example, if we collect all of the tweets of the official Twitter accounts of politicians in a country in addition to a selection of the public's tweets about politics, we can use the politicians' tweets as training data to construct what amounts to an affinity model. For example, Petrarca, Tyrberg, and Wilson (2019) use the Twitter accounts of Swedish politicians as the training data in which the output variable is which of the seven political parties the politician belongs to. This then is applied to public tweets to classify each tweet according to which party it most resembles, and to tweets by bots to identify patterns in which political platforms were being pushed disproportionately by foreign-operated bot accounts. Similar research designs can be applied wherever existing bodies of identifiable texts are available to train classifiers.

```
1  en_stop = set(stopwords.words('english'))
2  tweetsDB = "data/tweets.db"
3  labels = [0, 1]
4  num_categories = len(labels)
5  input_file = "nn"
6
7  model, dictionary = load_model(input_file)
8  tokenizer = Tokenizer(num_words=len(dictionary)+1)
9
10 tweets = []
11 conn = sqlite3.connect(tweetsDB)
12 c = conn.cursor()
13 for r in c.execute('SELECT id,text FROM tweets'):
14     tweet = TextTweet(r[0], r[1])
15     tweet.tokenize()
16     tweet.removeURLs()
17     tweet.removeStopwords(en_stop)
18     tweet.removeMentions()
19     tweet.removeShortwords(3)
20     tweet.text = ' '.join(tweet.words)
21     tweets.append(tweet)
```

```
22
23  for tweet in tweets:
24      text = prep_tweet(tweet.text, dictionary, tokenizer)
25      raw_pred = model.predict(text)
26      tweet.neuralnet = labels[np.argmax(raw_pred)]
27      q = (tweet.neuralnet, tweet.id)
28      c.execute("""UPDATE tweets SET neuralnet=? WHERE id=?""",q)
29  conn.commit()
30  conn.close()
```

Code Snippet 3.42 Appying a neural net model to out-of-sample tweets

Finally, we want to be able to take an existing neural net once we are satisfied with it, and apply it to additional out-of-sample tweets. Snippet 3.42 shows the main body of the file *neuralnet_apply.py*. It has a similar set up on lines 1–5 to match the neural net model we created in the last example. On line 7, it uses a helper function to load the model that we saved to files in the last example. Lines 13–21 implement the now familiar logic of grabbing tweets from the database, in this case *all* tweets from one of our tweets databases, and then running the text through our simplification methods. Finally, lines 23–28 loop through all of these tweets and apply the existing neural net to each tweet in turn, and then save the resulting prediction from the model to a field called "neuralnet" in the database.

3.4 Key Takeaways

This chapter covers a variety of ways to approach analyzing the content of social media data. It adds several data collection tools to your kit, including the ability to sample Twitter data on the basis of both keywords and languages, in addition to providing tools for accessing additional elements of content such as video, images, hashtags, mentions, and links. Finally, we cover a suite of tools for doing computer analysis of the text of tweets, using sentiment analysis, untrained latent topic modeling, and the implementation of neural nets in order to supervise the training of our own custom models.

4 Geospatial Analysis of Social Media Data

One of the most exciting types of social media data is geolocated data, which includes the exact latitude and longitude at the time of the posting to within a few meters, using the GPS capabilities of the posting device. This chapter discusses the particular advantages offered by this data, including the capacity to perform extremely fine-grained subnational studies impossible with traditional sources of data. In addition, the chapter provides software for processing geocoded social media data in order to efficiently identify the country and subnational unit of every tweet in a collection. Finally, the chapter concludes with a discussion of how to deal with the *location problem*, which is the difficulty of dealing with the small amount of geocoded data available, and how to generalize it to a larger population.

4.1 Data Availability

The integration of social media with the built-in GPS technology of many mobile devices has added exciting additional value to the available data. Twitter in particular has been a fruitful source of such geocoded data due to the early integration of the platform with mobile GPS. Approximately 1.5% of tweets worldwide have some type of geocoding attached and publicly available. This proportion has remained relatively constant over the last decade.

Snippet 4.1 shows an example block of JSON from a tweet that has been geocoded. Note that there are two fields ("coordinates" and "place") that would appear in the top level of a tweet's JSON, at the same level as "id" or the "user" object. If a tweet *isn't* geocoded, these two fields will either be empty, or in the case of some very old tweets (prior to 2009), missing entirely.

```
1    "coordinates": {
2      "type": "Point",
3      "coordinates": [-77.04310264,38.85701649]
4    }
5    "place": {
6      "country":"United States",
7      "country_code":"US",
8      "full_name":"Washington, DC",
```

```
 9│    "id":"01fbe706f872cb32",
10│    "name":"Washington",
11│    "place_type":"city",
12│    "url":"http://api.twitter.com/1/geo/id/0172cb32.json",
13│    "bounding_box": {
14│       "type":"Polygon",
15│       "coordinates": [[
16│          [-77.119759,38.791645],
17│          [-76.909393,38.791645],
18│          [-76.909393,38.995548],
19│          [-77.119759,38.995548]
20│       ]]
21│    }
22│ }
```

Code Snippet 4.1 Example of geocoded tweet

There are two types of geocoded tweets, which present differently in the JSON output from the Twitter application programming interface (API). The first type is *place-based* geocoding, which gives a predetermined latitude and longitude for a tweet based on a named place already in the Twitter database. The second is *precise* geocoding, which gives the exact latitude and longitude coordinates of the device at the time of posting.

The place-based geocoded tweets will always have a null "coordinates" field, while precise geocoded tweets will sometimes also have a place object defined, while sometimes leaving it null. Generally speaking, before 2015 precise tweets were unlikely to also have a defined place object, while from 2015 onward they were likely to do so. So if you explicitly want precise coordinates, be sure to look in the coordinates field; do not simply write code that assumes there are no coordinates if the place object is populated.

Place-based geocodes are assigned based on the user selecting when posting from a set of existing places that their location matches. The suggestions are based on the user's actual physical location, but nothing is technically stopping them from entering any location in the world. In addition, a user can potentially select from a variety of nested places in the Twitter database when at a given location. For instance, a user tweeting from the Empire State Building might instead select "Empire State Building," "Midtown," "Manhattan," "New York City," or "New York" state, among others.

These places have several categories that can behave slightly differently: admin, city, country, neighborhood, and point of interest. These values are stored in the "place_type" field of the place object in the JSON object for each tweet.

The first four are always defined with bounding boxes of latitude and longitude, i.e. a rectangle of GPS coordinates defining the rough area of that place.

Note that these bounding boxes should not be mistaken as having a probabilistic interpretation for a specific tweet. That is, the box's centroid is not the point estimate of the device's location, with the box itself being akin to a confidence interval around that estimate. Rather, the bounding boxes are deterministic: All tweets with a specific place assigned will have identical bounding boxes.

Lines 15–18 of the sample JSON illustrate the bounding box of the city of Washington, DC, with a set of four latitude/longitude coordinates. Note that all coordinates are listed as longitude, latitude rather than the traditional colloquial ordering. This is a convention in geographic information system (GIS) work because longitude represents the x-coordinate and latitude the y-coordinate, and so it's hewing to the mathematical convention of (x, y) ordering. Also note that while there are four points defined, it's really just the four permutations of two values of latitude and two values of longitude. Place boxes in the Twitter API are always rectangular, rather than being arbitrary polygons.

The size of these boxes varies extraordinarily, as one can imagine with places defined for everything from neighborhoods to entire countries. Table 4.1 shows the total distinct number of places of each type observed in geocoded tweets during the entirety of 2018 and 2019.

"Admin" corresponds to various subnational administrative units such as provinces, districts, or states, but should not be considered to be complete unless vetted on a country-by-country basis. For instance, the United States only has a few dozen entries in the "admin" database (including all 50 states), while there are several thousand admin entries for Russia (down to the *raion*/county level), but there are no observed entries for Ukraine at all.

The same applies for the other categories, which have been haphazardly and nontransparently added to over the years. For example, only 27 countries have any neighborhoods defined, and 55% of them are in India, Mexico, and Austria. The United States has over 15 000 cities defined as places, but only 4 200 neighborhoods (mostly in Southern California and New York City).

Table 4.1 Place types and total counts

Place Type	Count
Admin	8 385
City	174 701
Country	253
Neighborhood	76 243
Point of Interest (precise)	5 750 348
Point of Interest (box)	10 153

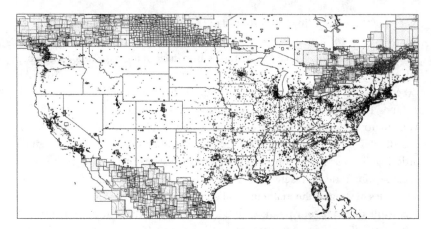

Figure 4.1 City and neighborhood place boxes in Twitter database, North America

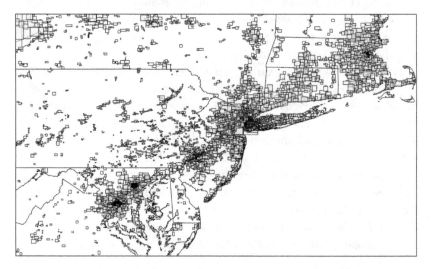

Figure 4.2 City and neighborhood place boxes in Twitter database, Northeast United States

Figure 4.1 shows all observed place boxes in North America of the city or neighborhood place types. Note the dramatic national variation in how places are defined, with Canada and Mexico having many "cities" defined with massive and overlapping boxes, while the United States has much smaller boxes, with wide swathes of rural areas entirely empty. Figure 4.2 zooms in to the American Northeast, centered on New York City to illustrate the dense and overlapping nature of these place definitions.

Worldwide, the average size of the bounding box for a city in the database is 0.09 units of latitude by 0.12 units of longitude, or approximately 6 by 8 miles. However, as the maps suggest, there is a great deal of national variance, with cities in the United States being about a quarter the size of the world average, and Canada's being three times the average. Neighborhoods are a bit smaller, on average only about 3 by 3 miles.

"Points of interest" come in two flavors: boxed and precise. A small fraction (about 10 000) have bounding boxes like other place types. They appear to be idiosyncratically defined, only originating from within nine countries (Austria, Estonia, Hungary, Indonesia, Lithuania, Malaysia, Poland, Portugal, and South Africa), with over 98% of them originating from Indonesia and South Africa. These are likely data inconsistencies and can probably be safely ignored as a phenomenon in your work. The vast majority of points of interest though are precise points instead of bounding boxes.

The second type of geocoded tweet is precise geocoding. These tweets self-report a precise latitude and longitude by the GPS functionality of the device itself, which is then listed in the Twitter API's output. These are precise latitude and longitude coordinates, estimated by the Federal Aviation Administration to be generally accurate to within three meters. Locations for this content can therefore be used at a much finer resolution than the national or regional levels usually available for social science research. Combined with time stamps accurate to the second, precision geocoded tweets can be used to observe events moment by moment and street by street.

However, these precise geocoded tweets require some historical context to understand their numbers. Originally, when GPS integration was first added to Twitter, users who opted in for it on their device automatically had all tweets assigned GPS coordinates. In May 2015, this policy was changed so that users had to choose to geocode on a per-tweet basis (Lapowsky, 2019). This led to a plummeting of precisely geocoded tweets at that point. While in May 2015 there were typically around 2.5 million precisely geocoded tweets worldwide per day, by 2017 that number had dropped to around 350 000. On the other hand, place-coded tweets grew drastically thanks to the interface change, reaching approximately three million per day.

A second change was announced in June 2019, when Twitter announced it would be disabling the assignment of precise geocodes to tweets unless the tweet contained an uploaded image (Twitter, 2019). However, tweets could still be precise geocoded via third-party apps. In the year since the announcement, however, there has not been a decrease in the number of tweets worldwide with precise coordinates attached, so it remains to be seen what the effect will be.

This history is relevant for two reasons. First, it is important to realize that data definitions and access can change over time, and so any current description

Table 4.2 Counts and types of geocoded tweets worldwide (February 1, 2020)

Geocoded Type	Count	% Total
Admin	395 370	9.83
City	3 120 916	77.57
Country	127 582	3.17
Neighborhood	12 909	0.32
Point of Interest	101 739	2.53
Total Place Coded	*3 758 516*	*93.42*
Precise Coded	264 749	6.58

will be transient. Second, these changes are not retroactive. If you download tweets now from these prior periods using the previously discussed methods of timeline scraping or downloading lists of ids compiled by other researchers, the data will be in its original form.

The total number of geocoded tweets streamed worldwide on a daily basis in 2020 are broken down into their type of geocoding in Table 4.2. At this point, 93% of tweets are place-coded, and of those the vast majority are geocoded at the city level.

The vast amount of tweets, and the long history of gradual changes to the available data, means that there are occasional quirks in the data. Researchers should keep this in mind and be prepared to adjust when unexpected idiosyncrasies arise in the data. For instance, from approximately midnight to seven a.m. GMT on January 26, 2018, all GPS tweets had their latitude and longitude coordinates transposed in the output from the streaming API.

A more long-term example was the fact that prior to the summer of 2015 (when the problem was apparently resolved) there are a significant quantity of GPS-enabled tweets pinpointed at the latitude/longitude coordinates of exactly 0.0, 0.0. This is about 375 miles off the coast of Ghana in the middle of the Atlantic Ocean and clearly is a data integrity error despite representing some 21 million tweets from 2012 to 2015. Due to that point's location, any bounding box that tries to capture Africa will also grab those tweets. See Kashmir Hill's 2019 piece in Gizmodo for a number of other examples of GPS databases causing issues for individuals who happened to live at chronically incorrectly propagated coordinates (Hill, 2019).

The level of geocoding also exhibits a great deal of geographic variation both from country to country and region to region. Experiments on collecting full language corpuses – especially those that are largely centered on certain countries like Swedish or Farsi – show a great deal of variance. While worldwide about 1.5% of tweets are estimated to be geocoded (roughly the proportion we see in the United States and Latin America), only about 1% of tweets from France are, while Nordic countries see rates closer to 3%.

4.2 Collecting Geocoded Data from Twitter

Downloading geocoded tweets is not particularly different from the other streamers we have set up previously. In fact, since geocoding is a standard part of the JSON object for downloaded tweets, you have already inevitably downloaded some geocoded tweets in the earlier chapters.

The key issue upfront is that Twitter's streaming API only allows you to either filter on geocodes or keywords. That is, the API itself cannot directly search for a term and a location. This section is for setting up a streamer dedicated to only downloading geocoded tweets. A modification of our streaming downloader is presented in Snippet 4.2, set up to download all tweets from a rectangle corresponding to the continental United States. Notice that this is almost identical to the keyword streamer presented previously. The only change is in replacing the array of keywords with an array of coordinates. Lines 4 through 7 set up several different latitude/longitude boxes for your convenience, although the code only uses the last one. Simply swap out the array referenced in line 17 to a different one, or create your own, for a different box. The order of coordinates is: [western longitude, southern latitude, eastern longitude, northern latitude].

```
1  from Streamer import Streamer
2
3  # Variable definitions
4  box_world = [-180,-90,180,90]
5  box_western_hemisphere = [-180,-90,-30,90]
6  box_eastern_hemisphere = [-30,-90,180,90]
7  box_continental_usa = [-130,24,-66,50]
8  output_dir = "queues"
9
10 auth_handler = OAuthHandler(consumer_key, consumer_secret)
11 auth_handler.set_access_token(access_token, access_token_secret)
12 api = API(auth_handler)
13
14 listener = Streamer()
15 listener.initQueue(output_dir, 3600, 'geo')
16 stream = tweepy.Stream(auth=api.auth, listener=listener)
17 stream.filter(locations=box_continental_usa)
```

Code Snippet 4.2 Geocoded streamer

Nothing is stopping you from entering latitude and longitude bounds that cover the entire planet (i.e. −90 to 90 and −180 to 180, as referenced in line 4 of the code). However, doing so will generally exceed the 1% cap of tweets you can stream at any given time (since geocoded tweets are roughly 1.5% of all tweets), which will lead to you receiving a randomly truncated set of tweets. If you need to download all the geocoded tweets in real time, simply set up multiple streams, carving up the surface of the globe into smaller sections. From experience, simply running a streamer for each hemisphere (the boxes defined in lines 5 and 6) will generally stay below the cap, other than during occasional spikes in traffic. However, for most applications, even for large areas such as the entire United States, the total number of geocoded tweets will consistently be under the 1% cap.

As with previous downloaders, this program will save the JSON of matched tweets to files inside the "queues" directory for later processing. A new file is rotated out every hour (thanks to the 3 600 seconds specified on line 15) so there will be 24 files with time stamps for names each day.

Next, let's set up the code needed to support the geocoded elements of the tweets in our database and software infrastructure. First, Snippet 4.3 sets up a database with additional fields to store the geocoded information for each tweet, in addition to a table to hold data about the places that are defined in the tweets. The tweets table is very similar to the ones we have set up previously, with just the addition of fields for latitude and longitude (*float* means a decimal number in this context), the associated place_id (unlike most identifier fields, place ids are alphanumeric, not integers), and a field called "geo_type" that we will use to specify whether the tweet in question has precise or place-based geocoding. In addition we include a "country" field in anticipation of calculating the country of origin of each tweet later in the chapter.

```
 1 import sqlite3
 2
 3 conn = sqlite3.connect("data/data.db")
 4 c = conn.cursor()
 5 c.execute('''CREATE TABLE tweets (
 6             id BIGINT,
 7             created DATETIME,
 8             text VARCHAR,
 9             user_id BIGINT,
10             screen_name VARCHAR,
11             lat FLOAT,
12             lon FLOAT,
13             place_id VARCHAR,
14             geo_type VARCHAR,
15             country VARCHAR
16         )''')
17 c.execute('''CREATE UNIQUE INDEX idx_id ON tweets(id)''')
18 c.execute('''CREATE TABLE places (
```

```
19              id VARCHAR,
20              place_type VARCHAR,
21              name VARCHAR,
22              country_code VARCHAR,
23              lat_1 FLOAT,
24              lon_1 FLOAT,
25              lat_2 FLOAT,
26              lon_2 FLOAT,
27              country VARCHAR
28          )''')
29 c.execute('''CREATE UNIQUE INDEX idx_place_id ON places(id)''')
30 conn.commit()
31 conn.close()
```

Code Snippet 4.3 Geocoded database setup

The places table holds several key fields about places: the type, the name, the two-letter country-code, the latitude and longitude pairs that form the place box, and a second country field. This second field is to store the three letter-country code most common in GIS applications, as opposed to the two-letter field that Twitter internally attaches to all places.

In order to support places, we set up a Place object as shown in Snippet 4.4. The object has two methods: *loadJSON* pulls the appropriate values for each database field out of the JSON associated with a place, while *insert* saves an instantiated place into the database table for places that we just set up.

```
1  class Place:
2      def __init__(s, id):
3          s.id = id
4
5      def loadJSON(s, p_json):
6          s.place_type = p_json['place_type']
7          s.name = p_json['full_name']
8          s.country_code = p_json['country_code']
9          s.lat_1 = p_json['bounding_box']['coordinates'][0][0][1]
10         s.lat_2 = p_json['bounding_box']['coordinates'][0][2][1]
11         s.lon_1 = p_json['bounding_box']['coordinates'][0][0][0]
12         s.lon_2 = p_json['bounding_box']['coordinates'][0][2][0]
13
14     def insert(s, c):
15         q = (
16             s.id, s.place_type, s.name, s.country_code,
17             s.lat_1, s.lat_2, s.lon_1, s.lon_2, s.country
18         )
19         c.execute(
20             """REPLACE INTO places
21             (id, place_type, name, country_code,
22             lat_1, lat_2, lon_1, lon_2, country)
23             VALUES(?,?,?,?,?,?,?,?,?)""", q)
```

Code Snippet 4.4 Place object

Next, we modify the *BasicTweet* object with the additional helper methods shown in Snippet 4.5 for extracting the geocoded fields from a particular tweet's JSON (*getGeo*) and then inserting those fields into the database (*insertGeo*). Lines 2 through 6 set up default values for all of the geocode-related fields, so that if a nongeocoded tweet passes through this processor, they're stored with correct empty values. If a place is defined in the tweet's JSON, lines 10 and 11 will use the Place object we just set up, and in the tweet's insertion method, the place is inserted in lines 28 and 29.

```
 1    def getGeo(s):
 2        s.lat = None
 3        s.lon = None
 4        s.place_id = None
 5        s.place = None
 6        s.geo_type = "not"
 7        if 'place' in s.json and s.json['place'] is not None:
 8            s.geo_type = 'place'
 9            s.place_id = s.json['place']['id']
10            s.place = Place(s.place_id)
11            s.place.loadJSON(s.json['place'])
12        if 'coordinates' in s.json and s.json['coordinates'] is not None:
13            s.geo_type = 'precise'
14            s.lat = s.json['coordinates']['coordinates'][1]
15            s.lon = s.json['coordinates']['coordinates'][0]
16
17    def insertGeo(s, c):
18        q = (
19            s.tweet_id, s.created, s.user_id,
20            s.screen_name, s.text, s.lat, s.lon,
21            s.place_id, s.geo_type
22        )
23        c.execute(
24            """REPLACE INTO tweets
25            (id, created, user_id, screen_name, text,
26            lat, lon, place_id, geo_type)
27            VALUES(?,?,?,?,?,?,?,?,?)""", q)
28        if s.place:
29            s.place.insert(c)
```

Code Snippet 4.5 Geocoded tweet processing methods

Finally, Snippet 4.6 modifies our tried and true JSON processor to use these new methods (the existing code that parses the JSON is identical to previous instances and is not included here). Lines 1 through 7 open a comma-delimited file provided in the source code that contains a mapping of all the two-letter country codes to three-letter ones used in GIS applications for convenience. You should not have to modify that source file unless a new country comes along. This mapping is used in the database insertion steps on lines 14 through 17 by looking up the matching three-letter code for each tweet where a place is defined and saving it to the place's "country" field. If additional functionality that we developed earlier like image or video extraction is needed for the application, those methods can be called here as well.

```
1  # load country code mapping
2  c_codes = {}
3  df = pd.read_csv("c_codes.csv", encoding='UTF-8')
4  i = 0
5  for c_code in df['c_code']:
6      c_codes[c_code] = df['gid_0'][i]
7      i += 1
8
9  # Write those tweets to a database file
10 conn = sqlite3.connect(database)
11 c = conn.cursor()
12 for tweet in tweets:
13     tweet.getGeo()
14     if tweet.place:
15         tweet.place.country = None
16         if tweet.place.country_code in c_codes:
17             tweet.place.country = c_codes[tweet.place.country_code]
18     tweet.insertGeo(c)
19 conn.commit()
20 conn.close()
```

Code Snippet 4.6 Geocoded database insertions

At this point, we have set up a system for downloading geocoded tweets en masse, and inserting them into our database. Next, we'll turn to what we can actually do with this geocoded data.

4.3 Processing Geocoded Tweets

So we now have the ability to download and store geocoded tweets, but we also need to develop techniques for using that geocoding in research. The primary way of doing so is aggregating those tweets up to a level that can be joined with other social science data, typically to administrative units such as countries or smaller subnational units. To do this, we use shape files, which are databases of latitude/longitude coordinates defining shapes on a map. While an amazing variety of shape files are available, detailing everything from bodies of water to individual buildings to railroad lines, we will focus on ones that define territorial borders.

While there are a variety of different file formats (Google Earth's KMZ format, and the increasingly popular Geopackage format), we will use the ESRI shape file, a commonly used open format. Each shape file has the same basic design that is conceptually similar to a spreadsheet. In a shape file of the world's countries, each row corresponds to a single country, with metadata columns such as the country's name. An additional column contains an array of latitude/longitude coordinates that when connected (like a child's connecting-the-dots worksheet) define the shape of the country as a many-pointed polygon. Shape files can be truly massive since the complex borders of countries, especially their coastlines, require many individual points to be rendered accurately.

Luckily for us, geographers do the difficult work of actually producing shapefiles, and our task in this chapter is reduced to making use of them with our sets of Twitter coordinates. The Global Administrative Areas (GADM) project provides high-resolution shapefiles for all countries and their subnational units to variable levels (available at https://gadm.org) (GADM, 2020). In many countries, electoral districts are distinct from administrative boundaries, and shapefiles are often available through the electoral management boards or census bureaus. For example, shapefiles for the congressional districts of the United States can be downloaded from http://data.gov (Data.gov, 2020).

For this section, you will need to download the full world country borders shapefile from GADM, and unzip the archive in a convenient location on your computer. Please note that this is a very large set of files, taking up nearly four gigabytes of space when uncompressed. There will be a set of files called "gadm36_0" with several different file extensions. These are the country border files, while the files with different numbers in place of the zero (i.e. "gadm36_1," "gadm36_2," etc.) correspond to the first subnational level of administrative borders (i.e. state or province equivalent), second subnational, and so on. Note that while all countries are defined at the national and first subnational level, not all are represented at lower levels of subnational division. The "36" may also vary depending on when you download it as that indicates the version number of the shape files (in this case 36 indicates version 3.6 of the data). For country-specific applications, you can also download shapefiles that are just for specific countries.

As a first example, let's identify the country of origin for each tweet, using a point-in-polygon function to determine which polygon (i.e. country) our point happens to be inside. Point-in-polygon functions at their simplest take a given latitude/longitude point and a polygon formed by other latitude/longitude coordinates and calculate whether the point is inside the polygon in question. With country borders being defined by such complex polygons, these calculations are simple but very resource intensive for a computer. We will walk through building an infrastructure that utilizes a number of tricks to make the task of calculating country of origin for millions of tweets efficient enough to run on normal desktop computers.

Throughout this section, we will use new functions that have been included in the file *functions_geo.py* in the top level directory of the sample source code. Snippet 4.7 is the first of these, a simple function that takes in a database connection, tweet id, and country as inputs, and saves them to our database.

```
1 def save_country(c, id, country):
2     q = (country, id)
3     c.execute("""UPDATE tweets SET country = ? WHERE id=?""", q)
```

Code Snippet 4.7 Saving a tweet's country to the database

The simplest algorithm for identifying the country of origin for a set of our tweets is the file *geo_country.py*, detailed in Snippet 4.8. On the first two lines it imports the new functions file in addition to a new Python library called *shapefile*, which includes a number of important GIS tools we will be using. On line 6, we use this new library to open the shapefile that contains the borders of all the world's countries. You should modify this line to point at the equivalent file's location on your computer. Next, we connect to the database of tweets, select all the precise geocoded tweets with no country yet defined, and loop through them. On line 13, we call the function *scanBruteForce*, passing it the shapefile we just loaded along with the latitude and longitude of this particular tweet. Finally, we save each tweet's identified country to the database on line 14.

```
1 from functions_geo import *
2 import shapefile
3
4 # Variable definitions
5 inputDB = "data/data.db"
6 sf = shapefile.Reader(shapefile_dir+"gadm36_0.shp")
7
8 conn = sqlite3.connect(inputDB)
9 c = conn.cursor()
10 c.execute("SELECT id, lat, lon FROM tweets WHERE country IS NULL AND geo_type
      ='precise'")
11 for r in c.fetchall():
12     (id, lat, lon) = r
13     country = scanBruteForce(sf, lat, lon)
14     save_country(c, id, country)
15     conn.commit()
16 c.close()
17 conn.close()
```

Code Snippet 4.8 Identifying country of origin for precise geocoded tweets

Snippet 4.9 shows how *scanBruteForce* works. First, it uses our GIS library in order to create a *Point* object out of the latitude and longitude of our tweet. It then loops through all the countries in the shapefile we passed the function, and checks to see if the polygon corresponding to that country contains this particular point inside it. If it does, the function exits and returns the three-letter country code associated with that polygon (GID_0). If it finishes looping through all the countries and the point was not in any of them, it instead returns "NOT," our own three-letter code to indicate it was *not* matched.

```
1  def scanBruteForce(sf, lat, lon):
2      point = shapely.geometry.Point(lon, lat)
3      for country in sf.shapeRecords():
4          polygon = shapely.geometry.asShape(country.shape)
5          if polygon.contains(point):
6              return country.record['GID_0']
7      return 'NOT'
```

Code Snippet 4.9 Brute-force scanning of shapefiles

This is very simple code, and it works, but it will work *extraordinarily* slowly. If tweets are randomly distributed through the countries of the world (which of course they're not), on average this code would have to check over a hundred polygons for each tweet before finding the correct one. While computers run at vastly different speeds and so the time it takes to run code will vary dramatically, it can be illustrative in relative terms to provide some example times. On my desktop computer, which is on the high end of desktops, but certainly doesn't cross into the realm of heavy-duty server hardware, a random sample of tweets from around the world averages about two minutes to find the country of origin for each tweet. Russia's borders and coastline make its polygon so complicated that it alone takes 15 seconds per tweet. If we wanted to use this brute force function to find the country of origin for every precisely geocoded tweet in the world, each day's tweets would take about a year to process. So unless we have a *very* limited number of tweets to analyze, we probably want to introduce some more intelligent code.

4.3.1 Caching Coordinates

The first trick we can use is to realize that many tweets come from *exactly* the same coordinates, most commonly when someone posts several tweets at the same time having not moved. This certainly isn't the bulk of tweets, but it's a simple matter to make sure that if we have *already* calculated which country a particular set of coordinates is in that we don't bother doing it again.

```
 1  from functions_geo import *
 2  import shapefile
 3
 4  # Variable definitions
 5  inputDB = "data/data.db"
 6  sf = shapefile.Reader(shapefile_dir+"gadm36_0.shp")
 7  exact_hash = {}
 8
 9  conn = sqlite3.connect(inputDB)
10  c = conn.cursor()
11  c.execute("SELECT id, lat, lon FROM tweets WHERE country IS NULL AND geo_type
        ='precise'")
12  for r in c.fetchall():
13      (id, lat, lon) = r
14      key = str(lat) + '_' + str(lon)
15      country = 'NOT'
16      if key in exact_hash:
17          country = exact_hash[key]
18      else:
19          country = scanBruteForce(sf, lat, lon)
20      save_country(c, id, country)
21  c.close()
22  conn.close()
```

Code Snippet 4.10 Introducing exact caching

Snippet 4.10 shows the file *geo_country_exact.py*, which modifies our previous brute force code slightly. In line 7 it sets up an empty hash called *exact_hash*, which will store the country of each set of coordinates as we go. On line 14, we string together the latitude and longitude as key for that hash. We then check to see if that key is already in our hash, and if so we just use the country we already calculated. If not, on line 19 we go about using the brute force scanner from before. On average, this will only save us the trouble of calculating the country for 5–10% of the tweets and so doesn't solve the overall problem, but since it's trivial to implement it's an enhancement worth incorporating.

4.3.2 Guessing the Right Country

The problem with the brute force method of scanning all of the country polygons until we find the correct one is that it spends a lot of time searching the *wrong* polygons. By default what we have written above searches the polygons in the order they appear in the shapefile, which just happens to be alphabetical order. While it's a simple design, it has some relatively glaring flaws. For example, it's probably not a very *efficient* design that checks if a tweet originates from within the United States (source of a quarter of the world's geocoded tweets), only after checking 233 other country-polygons first. In this section, we implement a guessing strategy based on caching the country that was the "right" polygon for similar latitude/longitude coordinates for previous tweets.

While there is a decent amount of code in this section, its logic is relatively straightforward. First, we round off the latitude and longitude coordinates of the tweet to the nearest integer value. Second, we check a cache for what countries that rounded-off set of coordinates has matched to previously. Third, we check to see if the unrounded coordinates are in each of those countries first of all. Fourth, if and only if it didn't match, we check the rest of the world's shapes using the brute force method. Fifth, we update our cache so that in the future our guesses will be even more accurate.

Snippet 4.11 shows how to create a new cache database and table. Notice it creates a table that has a country (which will contain the three-character country code used in shapefiles) and integer values for latitude and longitude since those will only be used in rounded-off form in this table. It also has a "total" column, which will track how many times that set of rounded-off coordinates matched the given country. This has the value of allowing us to first search the more likely country when a particular set of rounded-off coordinates can match more than one country. In addition, on line 11 we create a unique index for the combination of latitude, longitude, and country.

```
1  import sqlite3
2
3  conn = sqlite3.connect("cache_new.db")
4  c = conn.cursor()
5  c.execute('''CREATE TABLE cache (
6              country VARCHAR,
7              lat INT,
8              lon INT,
9              total INT
10             )''')
11 c.execute('''CREATE UNIQUE INDEX idx_cache ON cache (lat,lon,country)''')
12 conn.commit()
13 conn.close()
```

Code Snippet 4.11 Creating a cache mapping coordinates onto likely countries

If you start with an empty cache, it will gradually fill out as you run tweets through the code in this section, being indistinguishable from brute force scanning initially but accelerating as more and more coordinates are added to the cache to allow it to guess better. However, to jump-start the process for you, the book's source code contains a file called *cache.db* that is the result of having run this code against about 250 million tweets from around the world. If you modify the code from this section to run against different shapefiles (for instance, identifying congressional districts or provinces instead of countries), your cache would need to begin populating from scratch.

```
1  inputDB = "data/data.db"
2  cacheDB = "cache.db"
3  sf = shapefile.Reader(shapefile_dir+"gadm36_0.shp")
4  exact_hash = {}
5  shape_hash = cacheShapes(sf)
6  cache = getCache(cacheDB)
7
8  conn = sqlite3.connect(inputDB)
9  c = conn.cursor()
10 c.execute("SELECT id, lat, lon FROM tweets WHERE country IS NULL AND geo_type
      ='precise'")
11 for r in c.fetchall():
12     (id, lat, lon) = r
13     key = str(lat) + '_' + str(lon)
14     country = 'NOT'
15     if key in exact_hash:
16         country = exact_hash[key]
17     else:
18         country, cache = scanCache(shape_hash, cache, lat, lon)
19         if country == 'NOT':
20             country, cache = scanFull(shape_hash, cache, lat, lon)
21     save_country(c, id, country)
22     conn.commit()
23 c.close()
24 conn.close()
25
26 updateCache(cacheDB, cache)
```

Code Snippet 4.12 Introducing best-guess caching

Snippet 4.12 shows how we can adapt our scanner to this new logic. It has the same basic form as the previous ones: It loads a shapefile, it selects tweets from the database, loops through those tweets, figures out which country the tweet is in, and then saves the result to the database.

```
1  # this function caches the shapes from a shapefile by country
2  def cacheShapes(sf):
3      country_hash = {}
4      for country in sf.shapeRecords():
5          polygon = shapely.geometry.asShape(country.shape)
6          c_code = country.record['GID_0']
7          country_hash[c_code] = polygon
8      return country_hash
```

Code Snippet 4.13 Caching the shapes

First, let's look at the function called on line 5: *cacheShapes*, which is shown in Snippet 4.13. This function takes as an input the shapefile we opened with the countries of the world, and returns a variable called *country_hash* that stores each polygon object keyed to the three-letter country code (GID_0). This will allow us to grab any country's matching polygon without needing to loop through all of them each time. That is, if we know that we want to check the USA polygon, we can jump right to it (by referencing *country_hash['USA']*) instead of looping through an array of country shapes each time. The reason that we put this logic into a function is so that we can pass any shapefile to it and get a similar hash of polygons, which will be important later in this chapter. Note that because the shapefile in question is over a gigabyte in size, just running this several-line function takes a couple of minutes on most desktop computers.

Next, let's look at the functions called on line 6 (*getCache*) and line 26 (*updateCache*). The former loads the values of the cache database we referenced earlier, while the latter saves any updated information to it. Snippet 4.14 shows how the cache is loaded, by connecting to the database and simply selecting everything from that cache table. Note that when selecting that table's contents though, it sorts the outputs specifically by the latitude and longitude, and then by the total count in descending order. That is, each of the particular latitude/longitude combinations will cluster together, but the most frequently matched countries for each combination will be listed first. We do this so that the country's polygons will be searched in the order of most to least likely to match. The end result of this function is a hash keyed to the rounded-off latitude/longitude combinations (the "key" in line 8), with an array of countries to search for each combination (lines 9 through 11). The individual items in that array are the country code, the current total number of matches, and a boolean called "changed" that is initially False.

```
1  # this function loads the cache of previous lat/lon/country matches:
2  def getCache(cacheDB):
3      cache = {}
4      conn = sqlite3.connect(cacheDB)
5      c = conn.cursor()
6      c.execute("SELECT lat, lon, country, total FROM cache ORDER BY lat, lon,
          total DESC")
7      for r in c.fetchall():
8          key = str(r[0]) + '_' + str(r[1])
9          if key not in cache:
10             cache[key] = []
11         cache[key].append({'c_code': r[2], 'total': r[3], 'changed': False})
12     c.close()
13     conn.close()
14     return cache
```

Code Snippet 4.14 Caching countries near each point

Snippet 4.15 is the function that runs at the end of our program, saving any changes to the cache to the database. It takes as an input the database file and the cache object we just loaded in the previous function. It loops through each lat/lon combination in that object (beginning on line 5) and then each individual country in the array associated with that combination (line 6). On line 7 it checks to see if the particular item has been marked as changed, and if not, skips it entirely. This is so that we only update the cache database on lines 10–11 when the values have actually changed.

```
1  # update the database cache
2  def updateCache(cacheDB, cache):
3      conn = sqlite3.connect(cacheDB)
4      c = conn.cursor()
5      for key in cache:
6          for country in cache[key]:
7              if country['changed']:
8                  lat, lon = key.split('_')
9                  q = (lat, lon, country['c_code'], country['total'])
10                 c.execute("""REPLACE INTO cache (lat, lon, country, total)
11                     VALUES (?, ?, ?, ?)""", q)
12     conn.commit()
13     c.close()
14     conn.close()
```

Code Snippet 4.15 Saving the updated cache to the database

Returning to our base program back in Snippet 4.12, we can get to the main logic of lines 18–20, in which two different functions are used to attempt to identify the country of origin for the tweet. First, we run *scanCache* on line 18, passing it the hash of polygons, the cache, and the tweet's precise latitude and longitude. The function is designed to *only* search the polygons the cache says have worked before, and returns both the identified country and the update version of the cache. Snippet 4.16 shows this function, which is very similar to the original brute force function we wrote, with a few tweaks.

```
1  def scanCache(shape_hash, cache, lat, lon):
2      key = str(int(round(lat))) + "_" + str(int(round(lon)))
3      log(key)
4      point = shapely.geometry.Point(lon, lat)
5      if key in cache:
6          for country in cache[key]:
7              log("Trying " + country['c_code'])
8              if country['c_code'] in shape_hash:
9                  polygon = shape_hash[country['c_code']]
10                 if polygon.contains(point):
11                     country['total'] += 1
12                     country['changed'] = True
13                     return country['c_code'], cache
14     return 'NOT', cache
```

Code Snippet 4.16 Scanning all likely countries

On line 2, it rounds off to the nearest integer the latitude and longitude, and creates a key that we can use with the cache we just set up. It checks on line 5 to see if this particular rounded-off set of coordinates appears in the cache and, if so, loops through the countries in the cache using the usual point-in-polygon functions we have already covered, pulling out each specific polygon as appropriate from our hash of shapes on line 9. In order to update our cache with additional information, if the polygon matches on line 10, before returning the identified country code to the main program, it first increments that total number of matches for this country-key by one in line 11 and then flags the record as having been changed in line 12. That way, when *updateCache* is run at the end of the base program, this particular record will be updated in the database.

```
1  # this function scans all countries, but also saves changes to cache
2  def scanFull(shape_hash, cache, lat, lon):
3      key = str(int(round(lat))) + "_" + str(int(round(lon)))
4      log(key)
5      point = shapely.geometry.Point(lon, lat)
6      for c_code in shape_hash:
7          polygon = shape_hash[c_code]
8          log("(Full) Trying: "+c_code)
9          if polygon.contains(point):
10             if key not in cache:
11                 cache[key] = []
12             cache[key].append({'c_code': c_code, 'total': 1, 'changed': True})
13             return c_code, cache
14
15     return 'NOT', cache
```

Code Snippet 4.17 Scanning all countries

Back on line 19 of the base program in Snippet 4.12, if the country code is still "NOT," i.e. the best guesses did not find a match, it goes ahead and runs *scanFull*, which is an updated version of our brute force function that integrates the cache. Seen in Snippet 4.17, it still loops through all of the shapes, but this time when it does find a match, it updates the cache on lines 10 through 12, so that every time a full scan is necessary, it's ideally only necessary *once* for that particular set of rounded-off coordinates.

The end result of this work on creating a cache is that once enough tweets have been run through the processor, the brute force scanner will almost never run, because the cache allows the program to check the most likely polygons first across the board. Running this code with the fully burned-in cache on a day's worth of all precise geocoded tweets in the world shows that 96% of tweets match to the first polygon they are tested against, 2% to the second, and 0.4% to the third or fourth. Only 1.6% of tweets need run through the brute force scanner. In terms of a performance increase, this code will be able to run a

Figure 4.3 Sample of tweets matching no country

day's worth of geocoded tweets in about 19 days of processing, an enormous improvement from the year of processing pure brute force scanning would take. In addition, about a third of the processing time is dedicated just to those 1.6% of tweets that require a full scan.

4.3.3 Fuzzy Matching for Coastlines

Figure 4.3 shows a map of Eastern Europe and the Middle East, with points representing the coordinates of all the tweets in that area from a single day that did not match *any* country using our scanner. Note that all of the points are scattered along coastlines, with a very large cluster in the Bosphorus Strait in Istanbul. This is a result of the mismatch between the precision of GPS coordinates and the shapefiles, such that a tweet near a coastline is marginally outside of the country's polygon. This can also happen with a relatively high frequency when tweets are posted from man-made structures over water (such as piers or bridges) that are not reflected in the administrative boundary shapefiles.

To correct for this, in Snippet 4.18 we introduce new versions of our cache and full scan functions that allow for some rounding error. Both functions are duplicates of their previous versions, with changes to two lines of code. First, on lines 5 and 21, instead of defining a Point object, we instead use the *buffer* method to generate a "rough Point," which is a circle centered on the tweet's latitude and longitude with a radius of 0.1 units of latitude/longitude (roughly a kilometer). Then, on lines 11 and 25, instead of checking to see if the polygon *contains* the point, we check to see if the polygon *intersects* with the circle to generate a match.

```
1  # scan cached countries only, with rough intersection logic
2  def scanCacheRough(shape_hash, cache, lat, lon):
3      key = str(int(round(lat))) + "_" + str(int(round(lon)))
4      log(key)
5      roughPoint = shapely.geometry.Point(lon, lat).buffer(0.1)
6      if key in cache:
7          for country in cache[key]:
8              log("Trying " + country['c_code'])
9              if country['c_code'] in shape_hash:
10                 polygon = shape_hash[country['c_code']]
11                 if polygon.intersects(roughPoint):
12                     country['total'] += 1
13                     country['changed'] = True
14                     return country['c_code'], cache
15     return 'NOT', cache
16
17 # scan full country list with rough intersection logic
18 def scanFullRough(shape_hash, cache, lat, lon):
19     key = str(int(round(lat))) + "_" + str(int(round(lon)))
20     log(key)
21     roughPoint = shapely.geometry.Point(lon, lat).buffer(0.1)
22     for c_code in shape_hash:
23         polygon = shape_hash[c_code]
24         log("(Full) Trying: "+c_code)
25         if polygon.intersects(roughPoint):
26             if key not in cache:
27                 cache[key] = []
28             cache[key].append({'c_code': c_code, 'total': 1, 'changed': True})
29             return c_code, cache
30
31     return 'NOT', cache
```

Code Snippet 4.18 Scanning all countries

Snippet 4.19 shows the changes to the base processor, which now calls the two "rough" functions after the cache and full scan functions if there still has not been a match. Approximately two-thirds of otherwise unmatched coordinates can be matched to a country with this technique.

```
1  inputDB = "data/data.db"
2  cacheDB = "cache.db"
3  sf = shapefile.Reader(shapefile_dir+"gadm36_0.shp")
4  shape_hash = cacheShapes(sf)
5  exact_hash = {}
6  cache = getCache(cacheDB)
7
8  conn = sqlite3.connect(inputDB)
```

```
 9  c = conn.cursor()
10  c.execute("SELECT id, lat, lon FROM tweets WHERE country IS NULL AND geo_type
          ='precise'")
11  for r in c.fetchall():
12      (id, lat, lon) = r
13      key = str(lat) + '_' + str(lon)
14      country = 'NOT'
15      if key in exact_hash:
16          country = exact_hash[key]
17      else:
18          country, cache = scanCache(shape_hash, cache, lat, lon)
19          if country == 'NOT':
20              country, cache = scanFull(shape_hash, cache, lat, lon)
21          if country == 'NOT':
22              country, cache = scanCacheRough(shape_hash, cache, lat, lon)
23          if country == 'NOT':
24              country, cache = scanFullRough(shape_hash, cache, lat, lon)
25      save_country(c, id, country)
26      conn.commit()
27  c.close()
28  conn.close()
29
30  updateCache(cacheDB, cache)
```

Code Snippet 4.19 Introducing rough matching

4.3.4 Simplifying the Search Further

The innovations so far have drastically improved the efficiency of our GIS calculations, but they still bottleneck on the sheer size and complexity of the shapes of the countries themselves. Even guessing the *correct* shape, coordinates take on average about five seconds to check against that country's shape. The solution to this is simplifying the shapes that we are checking. But this is easier said than done, because simplifying a shapefile means making it less detailed, and therefore taking the risk of misidentifying on which side of a border a particular point should be. Ideally, we would like simple versions of the shapes of each country, that nonetheless will report no false positives. Figure 4.4 shows an example of this, zoomed into Europe, with simple shaded shapes overlaying the detailed borders of the full country border shapefiles. Note that the simplified versions are completely contained within their parent countries, but manage with relatively few points to cover the vast majority of the land area of each country.

Snippet 4.20 shows the file *simplify_shape_file.py*, which generates the simplified shapefile that we see above. It opens two shapefiles on lines 1 and 2: the original GADM country borders shapefile, and a new one that this program will populate. Line 3 copies the structure of the GADM file (in terms of what fields such as country name are included). We also set up variables for the total land

Figure 4.4 Simplified shapes of countries

area of the shapes in our files on lines 4 and 5 so that we can precisely measure how well this process works. We then loop through all of the countries in the original shapefile and simplify each of them in turn in a few steps.

First, we take the existing shape and shrink it inward slightly using the same "buffer" method on line 17 that we previously used to make points larger for fuzzy matching. By supplying a negative number, the method instead deflates the shape in question. We set the parameters for this on lines 13–15 by taking the square root of the shape's area to give a rough idea of the shape's order of magnitude (i.e. we need to shrink Russia by more than Switzerland in absolute terms) and then multiplying it by 0.03. Three percent was established through trial and error as a reasonable proportion of deflation, and seems to function well as an assumption for a variety of different shapefiles of other administrative boundaries, such as electoral districts or subnational units. Next, on line 19 we run the "simplify" method, which smooths out the edges of a shape. The reason we do this *after* deflating the shape is so that the smoothing happens within the original borders. Finally, we double-check on line 20 that the newly simplified shape is entirely within the old boundaries, and if not, transform it on line 22 to being only comprised of points within the original using the "intersection" method. Using these settings, only a half dozen or so country shapes end up needing that double check.

```
1  sf = shapefile.Reader(shapefile_dir+"gadm36_0.shp")
2  simple_sf = shapefile.Writer(shapefile_dir+"simple_gadm36_0")
3  simple_sf.fields = sf.fields[1:]
4  areaOldTotal = 0
5  areaNewTotal = 0
6
```

```
 7  for country in sf.iterShapeRecords():
 8      startShape = shapely.geometry.asShape(country.shape)
 9      # calculate old areas:
10      areaOld = startShape.area
11      areaOldTotal = areaOldTotal + areaOld
12      # calculate tolerances:
13      tolerance = .03 * math.sqrt(areaOld)
14      if tolerance > 0.5:
15          tolerance = 0.5
16      # shrink shape inwards:
17      simpleShape = startShape.buffer(-1*tolerance)
18      # simplify borders of shape:
19      simpleShape = simpleShape.simplify(tolerance)
20      if not simpleShape.within(startShape):
21          try:
22              simpleShape2 = simpleShape.intersection(startShape)
23              simpleShape = simpleShape2
24          except Exception as e:
25              log(country.record['GID_0'])
26
27      # calculate new areas:
28      areaNew = simpleShape.area
29      areaNewTotal = areaNewTotal + areaNew
30      efficiency = 100 * areaNew / areaOld
31      if efficiency > 10:
32          simple_sf.record(*country.record)
33          simple_sf.shape(mapping(simpleShape))
34      log(country.record['GID_0']+": " + str(efficiency) + "%")
35
36  efficiencyTotal = 100*areaNewTotal/areaOldTotal
37  log("Total Efficiency of "+str(efficiencyTotal)+"%")
38  simple_sf.close()
```

Code Snippet 4.20 Creating a simple version of a shapefile

The remainder of the code keeps track of the efficiency of the simplification process, which is the percentage of the original shape's land area that is comprised by the simplified shapes. The end result is a simplified shapefile that is two thousand times smaller than the original file, but covers 82% of the same land area with no potential for false positives. This allows us to modify our scanner in Snippet 4.21, which adds two more scans to the algorithm: a cache scan using the simplified version on line 20, and a full scan of the simplified file on line 24. Since the functions we wrote originally for this process took as an input a hash of shapes, we can reuse them here, passing those functions either the simple or complex versions of the shapes as needed.

```
1  inputDB = "data/data.db"
2  cacheDB = "cache.db"
3  sf = shapefile.Reader(shapefile_dir+"gadm36_0.shp")
4  simple_sf = shapefile.Writer(shapefile_dir+"simple_gadm36_0.shp")
5  shape_hash = cacheShapes(sf)
```

```
 6  simple_shape_hash = cacheShapes(simple_sf)
 7  exact_hash = {}
 8  cache = getCache(cacheDB)
 9
10  conn = sqlite3.connect(inputDB)
11  c = conn.cursor()
12  c.execute("SELECT id, lat, lon FROM tweets WHERE country IS NULL AND
          geo_type='precise'")
13  for r in c.fetchall():
14      (id, lat, lon) = r
15      key = str(lat) + '_' + str(lon)
16      country = 'NOT'
17      if key in exact_hash:
18          country = exact_hash[key]
19      else:
20          country, cache = scanCache(simple_shape_hash, cache, lat, lon)
21          if country == 'NOT':
22              country, cache = scanCache(shape_hash, cache, lat, lon)
23          if country == 'NOT':
24              country, cache = scanFull(simple_shape_hash, cache, lat, lon)
25          if country == 'NOT':
26              country, cache = scanFull(shape_hash, cache, lat, lon)
27          if country == 'NOT':
28              country, cache = scanCacheRough(shape_hash, cache, lat, lon)
29          if country == 'NOT':
30              country, cache = scanFullRough(shape_hash, cache, lat, lon)
31      save_country(c, id, country)
32  conn.commit()
33  c.close()
34  conn.close()
35
36  updateCache(cacheDB, cache)
```

Code Snippet 4.21 Updating scanner for simple shapes

In terms of performance, the simplified shapes are scanned at a rate of about 1 600 shapes per second, a staggering increase from the average of 5 seconds per shape for the complex versions. Roughly 60% of geocoded tweets can be matched to country based on the simple shape of the country alone. This drops the time it takes our example computer to process a day's worth of geocoded tweets from the entire world to 10 days.

4.3.5 Subnational Matching

What if we have projects that involve aggregating tweets to a level other than the country level? Subnational analysis is an area where geocoded tweets can really shine since their precision is measured in meters rather than miles. All of the code we have written above can be recycled and slightly tweaked for these purposes. For space concerns, we will not demonstrate the specific code here, but will describe implementation.

For example, if one wanted to identify the state or province of origin for tweets instead of country, the first step is to download the province-level boundaries shapefile from GADM. This file contains 3 610 province-polygons, each with a unique column called "GID_1." Second, modify the code we wrote above to reference "GID_1" in each place where it currently references "GID_0." Third, create a new column in your database called *province* and create versions of the functions that save and read the country field to reference that new province field instead. The exact same procedure can be used to drop the resolution down to the county level ("GID_2") or to use an entirely different source of shapefiles like congressional districts in the United States. Of course, if your research project is only collecting data from a certain country in the first place, one can further make the process efficient by hardcoding the functions to only check shapes within the country in question and ignore any coordinates outside those shapes.

Counterintuitively, smaller units are actually *more* efficient than larger ones. That is, it's actually faster to determine the province of origin than it is to determine the country of origin when a fully populated cache is available, even though knowing the province by definition tells you the country. This is because if the resolution of the shapefile is held constant, the smaller shapes are geometrically simpler, and thus each individually can be checked with a point-in-polygon function more quickly. And since our work in this chapter revolves around guessing the correct polygon for each point in advance, that means that each point can be resolved faster, because the handful of polygons it does check, it does so more quickly. For example, while identifying country of origin for a day's tweets requires 10 days on our example computer, identifying the province of origin takes 1.2 days. Identifying the county of origin only takes 45 minutes.

The trade-off is that the cache becomes much more resource intensive, having to deal with over 45 000 polygons at the county level worldwide. This can be more intensive than moderate desktops can handle, although it's not an issue if you have access to more robust computing.

4.3.6 Matching Places

Place geocoded tweets are much easier to deal with than precise geocoded tweets since we only need to do any GIS calculations once for a given place, and then our work is already done for any other tweet that has the same assigned place.

Implementing country matching as we've done above for precise geocoded tweets is particularly easy since all places already come with a country code identified by Twitter. Next, we will illustrate how to identify the country of origin of all place-coded tweets in a database. In Snippet 4.22, we define a function called *getPlaces* that caches all of the place ids and their corresponding countries.

Next, in Snippet 4.23, we call that function on line 3, and then select all place-coded tweets from the database on line 7. We loop through the tweets and, if the place_id is defined, we save the corresponding country to the database for that tweet.

```
1  # cache the countries for all the places in the database
2  def getPlaces(inputDB):
3      places = {}
4      conn = sqlite3.connect(inputDB)
5      c = conn.cursor()
6      c.execute("SELECT id, country FROM places")
7      for r in c.fetchall():
8          places[r[0]] = r[1]
9      c.close()
10     conn.close()
11     return places
```

Code Snippet 4.22 Getting countries of places

```
1  # Variable definitions
2  inputDB = "data/data.db"
3  places = getPlaces(inputDB)
4
5  conn = sqlite3.connect(inputDB)
6  c = conn.cursor()
7  c.execute("SELECT id, place_id FROM tweets WHERE country IS NULL AND geo_type
       ='place'")
8  for r in c.fetchall():
9      (id, place_id) = r
10     if place_id in places:
11         save_country(c, id, places[place_id])
12     conn.commit()
13 c.close()
14 conn.close()
```

Code Snippet 4.23 Introducing place matching

Subnational matching of places is more complicated of course, but it follows a similar principle: We do any GIS matching on the places, and then simply apply the findings to the tweets with those places. In order to identify the origin of points of interest places, simply run their latitude and longitude coordinates through the same process we used above for precise coded tweets.

The places that are defined by boxes are more complicated though. A relatively efficient and effective algorithm is to take the four pairs of coordinates that define the place box, in addition to the central point of that box, and run all five sets through our process. If the five points are in agreement, that place is definitely fully inside the administrative unit in question. If we are willing to have some margin of error, for instance saying that if the majority of the points are in the same administrative unit we assume that is the correct one, we can capture even more.

To give some metrics here: worldwide, 83% of city place boxes (which themselves represent nearly 80% of place-coded tweets) have five point matches to provinces, 92% have four or five, and 99% have three or more point matches. County level has lower accuracy, since counties are smaller than provinces: 60% have five point matches, 74% four or five, and 86% three or more. But these numbers are a bit more accurate than they seem at face value because of the tendency of coastal cities to have bounding place boxes with points out in the water. About 5% of place boxes historically have at least one point over water.

If accuracy is paramount, hand-coding places to administrative units is also feasible, if tedious work, but can be made more efficient when used in conjunction with the algorithm above. That is, use the five-point process in your project and then hand-code any places that do not have five point matches.

4.4 Grid Cell Identification

Many substantive applications are better suited to aggregation to grid cells rather than to administrative boundaries. Grid cells are squares of latitude and longitude, such that the entire surface of the Earth is broken into equal-sized squares.

Grid cells are often useful when covariates of interest are derived from natural features rather than political ones. For instance, a vast corpus of environmental data is available globally by grid cell, including rainfall, ground cover, soil quality, and the like. For example, the Global Land Analysis and Discovery dataset has global data for percentage of bare ground per grid cell, at the resolution of 0.00025 degree squares of latitude and longitude, which corresponds to approximately 30 meter squares (Ying et al., 2017). This is at the very smallest of the range of resolutions, and most datasets are much larger, with many standardized to resolutions of 1 degree squares for simplicity.

More social scientifically oriented examples of datasets are ones that estimate GDP, the Human Development Index (HDI), and population per grid cell (Kummu, Taka, and Guillaume, 2018; Nordhaus et al., 2006), at various grid cell resolutions. NASA's Socioeconomic Data and Applications Center (SEDAC) hosts a variety of such gridded datasets, at various resolutions (SEDAC, 2020). Usually the root of this data is in cleverly estimating social variables based on phenomena that are physically observable from satellite imagery of the planet.

For instance, high-resolution nighttime satellite photos of the entire globe are readily available, including on a time series basis. The visible light is evidence of the combination of electricity and concentrated population, which can be used to estimate the economic activity in an area, and thus GDP.

Integrating our social media data with grid cell data is very simple, and much easier to accomplish than the identification of political unit of origin that we wrote in Section 4.3, since identifying the grid cell of a particular set of latitude and longitude coordinates is simply an exercise in rounding. Snippet 4.24 shows an example application (*export_grid.py*) that generates a complete grid cell map of the world in terms of number of tweets that originated from within each cell, assuming that the grid cells are one unit of latitude and longitude each.

On line 10, it selects all latitude and longitude from all tweets in the database, along with the coordinate boxes of any places associated with each tweet. It then loops through each tweet and processes it by rounding off the latitude and longitude to the nearest integer (lines 15 and 16) in the case of precise-coded tweets. If there is no precise latitude and longitude in the database, it instead looks at the latitude and longitude of the associated place box. However, since places can be of very large sizes, on line 18 we check whether the size of the place is less than two units of latitude and longitude. If it's bigger than that, we skip the tweet, so that we don't assign for instance the place associated with an entire country to a single grid cell. Otherwise, we simply take the average latitude and longitude of the place, and round it off to the nearest integer. Line 23 creates a key string out of the latitude and longitude (for example "23_37" for latitude 23, longitude 37) and then checks if we have already seen that key previously on line 24. If we have, it increments the count in that grid cell by one (since each time through the loop represents a single tweet) in line 25. Otherwise, it stores the initial value of 1 in that grid cell's entry on line 27.

```
1  # Variable definitions
2  inputDB = "data/data.db"
3  outputCSV = "output_grid.csv"
4  columns = ['grid_lat','grid_lon','total']
5  output = []
6  output_hash = {}
7
8  conn = sqlite3.connect("data/data.db")
9  c = conn.cursor()
10 for r in c.execute("""SELECT lat,lon,p.lat_1,p.lon_1,p.lat_2,p.lon_2
11                      FROM tweets t, places p where t.place_id=p.id"""):
12     grid_lat = None
13     grid_lon = None
14     if r[0] and r[1]:
15         grid_lat = int(r[0] + 0.5)
16         grid_lon = int(r[1] + 0.5)
```

```
17    elif r[2]:
18        if abs(r[4]-r[2]) < 2 and abs(r[5]-r[3]) < 2:
19            grid_lat = int(((r[2] + r[4]) / 2) + 0.5)
20            grid_lon = int(((r[3] + r[5]) / 2) + 0.5)
21
22    if grid_lat is not None:
23        key = str(grid_lat) + "_" + str(grid_lon)
24        if key in output_hash:
25            output_hash[key] += 1
26        else:
27            output_hash[key] = 1
28
29 for key in output_hash:
30     (grid_lat, grid_lon) = key.split("_")
31     ret = {
32         'grid_lat': grid_lat,
33         'grid_lon': grid_lon,
34         'total': output_hash[key]
35     }
36     output.append(ret)
37
38 output_pd = pd.DataFrame(output)
39 output_pd.to_csv(outputCSV, index=False)
```

Code Snippet 4.24 Exporting totals by gridcell

Finally, after looping through all the tweets, lines 29 through 36 then loop through all of the latitude/longitude combinations we found, and stores them into an array for exporting to a CSV file on lines 38 and 39. The end result is a CSV file with three columns (grid cell latitude, grid cell longitude, and a count), which can be merged externally onto whatever other grid cell-based data is available for your project. This logic can be adapted easily at this point for grid cells of different sizes, or to incorporate logic besides simply counting the total number of tweets.

4.5 Solving the Location Problem

One of the limitations of using geocoded social media data is that only a small proportion of it is actually geocoded. For example, only about 1.5% of the total number of tweets have geocodes, and Twitter has one of the highest rates among social media sites for such tagging. This raises the question of how we can generalize this data beyond the small subset of users geocoding their tweets. Luckily, the low proportion of geocoded content is not quite as limiting as it appears at face value, and understanding how that is the case can potentially give us some tools for multiplying that proportion.

First, retweets are by definition not geocoded. Whenever a user retweets another tweet, even if they add their own comment, and even if they have location identification enabled on their device, a retweet will never have an attached geocode. Curious if this was actually the case in practice, I searched my entire database of around five billion geocoded tweets for any instance of a tweet's text starting with "RT @*" and only found a few hundred, all clearly manually typed that way by hand. The reason for this rule is likely to avoid scenarios such as retweets of tweets speaking in the first person appearing at face value to have clearly incorrect geocodes. For instance, consider a celebrity tweeting "I'm in NYC and love it" and thousands of people retweeting it with their retweet having their own location attached.

However, since around 80% of tweets are retweets, that eliminates a huge proportion of tweets. That is, while only 1.5% of tweets are geocoded, that is only out of a possible maximum of roughly 20%. I.e. the true proportion of tweets that are geocoded is closer to 7.5% from a certain perspective.

Second, while only 1.5% of tweets are geocoded, that does not mean that only 1.5% of users geocode 100% of their tweets. In practice, many users geocode some of their tweets. For some research questions, this means that we can effectively multiply how many geocoded tweets we have by building geographic profiles at the user level and applying that profile to all of their tweets.

For example, let us say that we are interested in how people in different regions of Brazil talk about the environment. If we set up a streamer that collects all geocoded tweets from Brazil, we will be able to capture regional variance, but only a small percentage of the tweets (presumably) will have anything to do with the environment. If we set up a streamer that collects all tweets that match a certain set of keywords about the environment, we will be able to capture the desired speech, but only a small percentage (presumably around 1.5%) will be able to tell us about the regional variance.

However, if we set up both streamers, we can leverage the two for more information. We do so by collecting all of the geocoded tweets over a long period of time, identifying which region the majority of a user's tweets were geocoded from and assuming all of their nongeocoded tweets were also from that region.

There are of course limitations to this approach that may misidentify the region of origin for users. This may happen if the "regions" in question are sufficiently small that a significant number of individuals could be expected to be posting from multiple regions in the course of normal everyday usage. For instance, in the United States one might expect minimal numbers of users to regularly post from multiple states, but many users might easily post from multiple counties, especially in metro areas like Los Angeles that span multiple counties. If this is a concern, one might only consider geocoded tweets from outside normal working hours to see if the results change significantly. If they do, one should use a larger scale of region, or possibly merge together neighboring regions that exhibit high levels of overlap.

In addition, users who only have a small number of geocoded tweets, but a large number of nongeocoded tweets might be ones that only post geocoded tweets when outside their living area. For instance, tourists from around the world posting geocoded selfies from the Statue of Liberty. This can be compensated for to a degree by setting thresholds either of a minimum absolute number or percentage of geocoded tweets that must exist before "counting." There are no hard and fast rules here, but trial and error in order to determine how much the measurements are changing should be employed to evaluate whether decisions are robust.

This technique works with different efficiency in different countries, depending on the particular online behavior of the population. In particular, populations that favor social media usage via mobile devices as opposed to traditional desktop computers will perform better, because a higher proportion of the user base will have at least some geocoded messages at some point in time.

Table 4.3 shows a sampling of how well the technique works for different countries. In each case, all geocoded tweets from the country in question were collected for several months, in addition to all tweets matching a set of political keywords related to a substantive set of topics (generally electorally related) during the period in question.

Note that the United States jumps from about 1.4% of tweets being geocoded in the source data to over 16%, with roughly similar results for other developed countries like Norway, Sweden, Russia, and France. Brazil and Nigeria on the other hand – with very different levels of Twitter usage and internet penetration rates – see similar patterns of jumping from around 1.5% to 31% and 26%, respectively. This demonstrates that a simple approach of identifying a user's

Table 4.3 Geocoded tweets from selected countries

Country	Start Date	End Date	Matches/Day	% Geocoded	% Geocodable
Brazil	9/19/2018	1/3/2019	2 708 328	1.46	30.98
France	3/6/2017	7/7/2017	2 150 519	1.10	8.81
Iran	9/16/2019	2/3/2020	880 074	0.46	3.90
Nigeria	1/3/2019	3/23/2019	2 441 697	1.60	26.38
Norway	11/15/2017	6/26/2019	53 951	2.57	12.48
Russia	3/7/2019	2/3/2020	1 667 493	1.56	17.02
Sweden	6/18/2018	10/12/2018	344 196	2.90	16.70
United States	9/17/2018	8/31/2019	3 815 128	1.41	16.23

geographic origin can multiply the number of geocoded tweets by an order of magnitude, from 10 to 20 times depending on the idiosyncrasies of a particular country.

On the other hand, Iran tells a very different story. Note that it has a baseline geocoded rate of only 0.5%, less than a third the global average and, even when using this technique, falls short of 4% geocodable. Twitter has been banned in Iran since the Green Revolution and so activity from within the country is almost entirely via VPN or other obfuscating technology that would intrinsically avoid providing accurate geocoding to Twitter. We do know that the majority of these tweets are actually coming from within Iran due to observed patterns in the stream's magnitude during times when the Iranian regime shut down all external internet access in the country. During those shutdown periods, the number of Farsi-language tweets drops by about 75%, indicating that despite our lack of precise geocoding, the bulk of the tweets are indeed coming from within Iran.

Similar tests can be performed over the long run with regard to any country that has large-scale blanket internet shutdowns by the government. These shutdowns can be leveraged as natural experiments, and used to quantify the proportion of the stream that is coming from the target country, as opposed to externally from diaspora groups who might just be talking about the country without actually being present in the country.

The following code shows how to set up a basic algorithm identifying the likely geocode of nongeocoded tweets. Snippet 4.25 sets up a table for storing the total number of times each user tweeted from each country in our database of tweets.

```
1  import sqlite3
2
3  conn = sqlite3.connect("data/data.db")
4  c = conn.cursor()
5  c.execute('''CREATE TABLE geo_users (
6              id BIGINT,
7              country VARCHAR,
8              pct FLOAT
9          )''')
10 conn.commit()
11 conn.close()
```

Code Snippet 4.25 Setting up geocoded user table

Snippet 4.26 populates that table, by looping through every tweet in a particular tweet database with a geocode (line 9), and keeping track of how many times each user id tweeted from each country. In order to efficiently store what could be a massive amount of data, we use associative arrays with a key of the user id and country name (as defined on line 17). The end result of the block of code from lines 9 to 20 will be a hash of every user-country combination in our database. Note that if you have multiple sources of geocoded tweets you can wrap this code in a loop through the different tables. Lines 22 through 35 loop through each user id we found, and then for each of those loops through every country they ever tweeted from. It then identifies which country they tweeted from the most, what percent of their total tweets that represented, and then saves that country to the *geo_users* table in line 35. After this code runs, the table will contain the most frequent country every user with geocoded tweets tweeted from.

```
 1  # Variable definitions
 2  inputDB = "data/data.db"
 3  user_hash = {}
 4  sums_hash = {}
 5  country_hash = {}
 6
 7  conn = sqlite3.connect(inputDB)
 8  c = conn.cursor()
 9  for r in c.execute("""SELECT user_id, country FROM tweets
10                        WHERE geo_type IN ('precise','place')"""):
11      if r[1] is not None:
12          uid = str(r[0])
13          if uid not in user_hash:
14              user_hash[uid] = True
15          if r[1] not in country_hash:
16              country_hash[r[1]] = True
17          key = uid + '_' + r[1]
18          if key not in sums_hash:
19              sums_hash[key] = 0
20          sums_hash[key] += 1
21
22  for u in user_hash:
23      maxVal = 0
24      my_country = None
25      u_total = 0
26      for country in country_hash:
27          key = u + '_' + country
28          if key in sums_hash:
29              u_total += sums_hash[key]
30              if sums_hash[key] >maxVal:
31                  maxVal=sums_hash[key]
32                  my_country = country
33      pct = float(maxVal)/float(u_total)
34      q = (u, my_country, pct)
35      c.execute("""INSERT INTO geo_users (id,country,pct) VALUES (?,?,?)""", q)
36
37  conn.commit()
38  conn.close()
```

Code Snippet 4.26 Aggregating user tweets by country

Finally, Snippet 4.27 populates a nongeocoded database of tweets with the likely country of origin based on the users' other activity. In this case we are simply connecting to the same tweets database, but we could easily point to a completely different one (for instance, one of our keyword tweet databases from a previous section). Note that in line 8, we specifically only choose user-country combinations with a percentage higher than 50%; if a higher threshold is desired, it could be set here. Next, note that on line 19 when we update the existing tweets with geocodes we set the new *geo_type* to "guess" so we can tell which ones were identified this way, and which were natively populated from the Twitter API's geocodes. In addition, we only update records without an existing geocode, so that we don't overwrite those with precise and place-based geocodes already in the table.

```
1  # Variable definitions
2  inputDB = "data/data.db"
3  outputDB = "data/data.db"
4  updates = []
5
6  conn = sqlite3.connect(inputDB)
7  c = conn.cursor()
8  c.execute("SELECT id, country FROM geo_users where pct>=0.5")
9  for r in c.fetchall():
10     update = {'id': r[0], 'country': r[1]}
11     updates.append(update)
12 c.close()
13 conn.close()
14
15 conn = sqlite3.connect(outputDB)
16 c = conn.cursor()
17 for update in updates:
18     q = (update['country'], update['id'])
19     c.execute("""UPDATE tweets SET geo_type='guess', country = ?
20              WHERE user_id=? AND geo_type='not'""", q)
21 conn.commit()
22 conn.close()
```

Code Snippet 4.27 Geocoding non-geocoded tweets by user history

This is a very simple approach, which could be more sophisticated in a number of ways. First, the algorithm could be built on an actual statistical model instead of just assuming that the user's location is the one they post from the majority of the time. Second, further probabilistic work can be done using additional metadata from the tweets. For instance the user location field in the user profile could be used with a combination of fuzzy string matches and a place database such as the GeoNames open database in order to identify additional user locations. When used in conjunction with the user's time zone settings, language settings, and contextual clues in their tweets, a far more comprehensive picture can be estimated. This is especially true for sourcing data from other social media sites such as Reddit or Instagram, where exact geocoding is not available but additional metadata and context clues exist.

4.6 Key Takeaways

In this chapter, we have covered a lot of ground, but you should be well-positioned to take advantage of geocoded social media data, in particular the rich geocoded data available from Twitter. There are several key points to keep in mind. First, there is a prodigious amount of geocoded data available for collection (several million such posts just from Twitter every day), and that data has a nuanced history and complexity to it that should be understood in order to make proper use of it. Second, while there is an incredible amount of complexity to dealing with geocoded data, clever use of GIS technology can render the problems tractable even on your personal computer. Third, while geocoded data is a tiny fraction of the available data, there are tools for multiplying its coverage and compensating for the problems inherent in location data.

5 Network Analysis of Social Media Data

Social media data also frequently has elements that are amenable to network analysis, including friend/follower networks and retweets. This chapter addresses how to operationalize this data into measures appropriate for network analysis, along with presenting sample applications.

5.1 Getting Started with Networks

At their simplest, networks are descriptions of the connections between different items. A computer network is a set of computers that are connected to one another. A friend network is a set of people who are connected to each other via relationships.

Typically this is constructed mathematically by defining a *graph* (the more technical term for a network) composed of *nodes* and *edges*. Nodes are the items that can be connected, i.e. the computers or people in the previous examples. Edges are the connections themselves, i.e. the wires between computers or the specific relationships between people. In a social media context there are a variety of conceptual networks (or graphs) that can be constructed depending on our research question, and how it maps best onto nodes and edges.

The most straightforward way of constructing such a network is to define the nodes as individual users on social media, and the edges as the relationship between them. For example, if we took as our set of nodes all the members of Congress, we might define the edges as a dichotomous quantity of whether any two members follow each other or not, thus constructing a "friend" network of Congress. Of course, we could define the edges in any number of other ways as well: the number of followers the two have in common, the number of hashtags they have both used over the period of a study, etc.

In this chapter we will walk through a number of these examples, but first we need to set up a system for downloading the activity of individual Twitter users of interest. In previous chapters, we have used the streaming application programming interface (API) in order to collect tweets meeting either geographic or keyword criteria across the entire swath of the user base. Now we will discuss collecting data from specifically identified user accounts, and then use that data as a basis for network analysis.

5.2 Collecting Data by User

One of the primary ways that researchers download Twitter data is by identifying particular user accounts of interest and downloading *everything* that user posts. This holds true for data collected from any social media site. Whether it is Facebook, Instagram, or one of the blogging platforms, the most intuitive point of entry for collecting data is often at the particular user level. The Twitter API makes this easy to do with Twitter data, but with some significant caveats.

First, when you connect to the API and request all tweets by a particular account, it will only return up to the 3 200 most recent tweets on that user's timeline, regardless of how far back in time that cap of 3 200 allows. For many projects this can be more than enough, such as those directed at accounts with very little activity or over a short period of time. For instance, members of Congress tend to tweet on average 2.7 times per day (and every member of Congress does have a Twitter account at this point, as does every sitting American governor), which multiplies out to just shy of a thousand tweets per year. So *on average* that 3 200 limit allows a scholar to download all tweets for all members of Congress through the last congressional term with ease. However, high-volume users can cause potential issues. Representative Alexandria Ocasio-Cortez, famed for her social media prowess, tweeted on average 20 times per day during her first few months in office, meaning that a downloader could only get the last six months or so of her tweets. The Twitter feeds of news organizations are also a popular target for data collection, but those are especially high traffic. The *New York Times* Twitter account tweets a hundred times per day on average, meaning that account's tweets can only be scraped about a month back at any given point in time.

An additional caveat is that this approach will miss any tweets that the user deletes before you download them, that is, it can only download the tweets that are currently up on the site. This is true when looking at Twitter from a web browser as well, and is what had led to many Twitter users taking screenshots of offensive tweets by public figures before they can be deleted, in order to "keep the receipts," in internet slang.

Both of these caveats lead to the same recommendation for all social media data collection: *collect early and collect everything*. That is, since there is almost no resource cost to downloading more data than you need, start downloading your items of interest as early as possible and by casting as wide a net as possible.

It is easy to discard data you don't end up needing, but exceptionally difficult to get data after enough time has passed.

We will now walk through two ways to implement timeline downloading. The first (and simpler way) is to simply grab the entire timeline of several user accounts as a one-time operation. The second sets up a database tracking such downloading so that we can keep grabbing new tweets on the timelines as time goes on, thus tracking those user timelines for as long into the future as your project requires. The code in this section is all contained in the directory *02-Timeline*, in addition to appearing in the text.

5.2.1 A One-Time Timeline Downloader

First let's set up a program that downloads all tweets (or at least up to the 3 200 limit for each) that have been posted by a set of accounts. Snippet 5.1 shows a very simple CSV file (*accounts.csv* in the sample code) that only has one column (and hence contains no commas, ironically). You can create your own CSV file with accounts you'd prefer to download by simply creating a plain text file with the first line "screen_name" and each subsequent line being the name of an account you'd like to download. For this example, we have the official accounts of three sitting senators as of 2019.

```
1 screen_name
2 SenMarkKelly
3 SenSasse
4 SenRubioPress
```

Code Snippet 5.1 CSV file containing screen names to download

Snippet 5.2 shows *snag.py*, which builds upon our previous programs that downloaded tweets with a few variations in order to access the timeline portion of the Twitter API. Line 2 points at the CSV file containing the screen names to be downloaded, and lines 6 through 8 open that file and create a list called "accounts" in which each item is a screen name from the CSV file. The program then opens a connection to the Twitter API on lines 11 through 13 and the bulk of the logic is in the loop that starts on line 16, individually looping through each of the accounts.

Finally, lines 20 through 27 are the core command that grabs the tweets for a given account from Twitter so that we can process them on lines 29 through 32. You will notice that this set of code is extremely similar to the previous code for downloading tweets by unique id, with the only significant variations being lines 21, 22, and 23. Line 21 tells the program to connect specifically to the part of the API that deals with timelines, while line 22 specifies *which* account's tweets you want to download. Line 23 (*since_id*) indicates that you want to download tweets that have been posted to this timeline since that unique tweet id (recall that all tweets have their own unique integer, always counting upward) was posted. In this case, we specify a 1 (which would be the id of the very first tweet back in 2006) to indicate that we want each of these timelines back in time as far as we can.

```
 1 # Variable definitions
 2 inputFile = "accounts.csv"
 3 outputDir = "queues/"
 4
 5 # Grab list of screen names to download
 6 accounts = []
 7 df = pd.read_csv(inputFile,encoding='UTF-8')
 8 accounts = [x for x in df['screen_name']]
 9
10 # Connect to API
11 auth_handler = OAuthHandler(consumer_key,consumer_secret)
12 auth_handler.set_access_token(access_token,access_token_secret)
13 api = API(auth_handler)
14
15 # Loop through the screen names and download their tweets
16 for account in accounts:
17     outputFile = outputDir + account + ".json"
18     file = open(outputFile, 'w')
19     try:
20         tweets = Cursor(
21                         api.user_timeline,
22                         id=account,
23                         since_id=1,
24                         wait_on_rate_limit=True,
25                         monitor_rate_limit=True,
26                         tweet_mode="extended"
27                     )
28         counter=0
29         for tweet in tweets.items():
30             counter+=1
31             json.dump(tweet._json,file)
32             file.write("\n")
33         log("Downloaded "+str(counter)+" tweets from "+account)
34     except:
35         log("Error downloading tweets for account: "+account)
36     file.close()
```

Code Snippet 5.2 Basic timeline downloader

Note line 17 creates a new JSON file for each account (SenMarkKelly.json, SenSasse.json, and SenRubioPress.json) so that the tweets from each account are stored in their own specific file for ease of organization. These JSON files are saved into the *queues* directory that we set up last time. Each of these JSON files is structurally exactly the same as the files we downloaded previously: Each line corresponds to a single tweet, with a JSON structure as defined by the API. As such, these downloads can be processed using any of the processor programs we have written throughout the book.

5.2.2 An Infrastructure for Timeline Downloading

Section 5.2.1 showed how to download timelines as a one-off event for a project, but often our projects will require us to download tweets over the long haul. To do so we are going to create a database that tracks which tweets we have downloaded for each account and modify the downloader program so that it only grabs tweets for each account that have posted since the last time our downloader ran. First, we set up the database with Snippet 5.3, which creates a table called *accounts* and imports our previous CSV file listing screen names into it. The field *last_id* we initially set to 1 for each screen name.

```
1  # Variable definitions
2  inputFile = "accounts.csv"
3  timelineDB = "data/timeline.db"
4
5  # Set up database structure
6  conn = sqlite3.connect(timelineDB)
7  c = conn.cursor()
8
9  # Set up a table for accounts
10 c.execute("""CREATE TABLE IF NOT EXISTS accounts (
11              user_id BIGINT,
12              screen_name VARCHAR,
13              last_id BIGINT,
14              name VARCHAR,
15              follower_count INT,
16              friend_count INT,
17              status_count INT,
18              verified INT
19          )""")
20 c.execute('''CREATE UNIQUE INDEX IF NOT EXISTS
21              idx_screen_name ON accounts(screen_name)''')
22
23 # Grab list of screen names to download
24 accounts = []
25 df = pd.read_csv(inputFile, encoding='UTF-8')
26 accounts = [x for x in df['screen_name']]
27
28 for account in accounts:
29     q = [account]
30     c.execute("""REPLACE INTO accounts
```

```
31|                  (screen_name,last_id)
32|                  VALUES (?,1)""", q)
33|
34| conn.commit()
35| conn.close()
```

Code Snippet 5.3 Setting up database for timeline downloading

Next we snag tweets a little bit differently with the file *snag_db.py* in Snippet 5.4, which is very similar to the downloader in Section 5.2.1 with a couple of key differences. First, instead of getting the list of screen names from the CSV file, it gets them directly from the database table in the previous step, in lines 6 through 12. Next, notice lines 22 and 23 name the output JSON file a combination of the screen name and the current date and time. This is so that each time new tweets are downloaded, they are put into a new file for each account. So we don't have to worry about overwriting the previously downloaded tweets.

Finally, note that now in the call to Twitter's API, instead of passing a *since_id* of 1 on line 29, we instead tell it to get all tweets since the *last_id* associated with that screen name in our database. Of course, the first time this program is run, that will still be 1 for each screen name, but notice that on line 39, when we loop through the tweets and write them to a JSON file, we now keep track of what the maximum tweet id is for each screen name and then save that value to the accounts table in the next few lines. This means that the *next* time we run this downloader, it will only download the tweets that have been posted since the last one we grabbed for each specific user.

```
 1| # Variable definitions
 2| timelineDB = "data/timeline.db"
 3| outputDir = "queues/"
 4|
 5| # Grab list of screen names to download
 6| accounts = []
 7| conn = sqlite3.connect(timelineDB)
 8| c = conn.cursor()
 9| for r in c.execute("SELECT screen_name, last_id FROM accounts"):
10|     account={'screen_name':r[0], 'last_id':int(r[1])}
11|     accounts.append(account)
12| conn.close()
13|
14| # Connect to API
15| auth_handler = OAuthHandler(consumer_key,consumer_secret)
16| auth_handler.set_access_token(access_token,access_token_secret)
17| api = API(auth_handler)
18|
19| # Loop through the screen names and download their tweets
20| for account in accounts:
21|     last_id = 1
22|     now = datetime.datetime.now().strftime(".%Y%m%d-%H%M%S")
23|     outputFile = outputDir + account['screen_name'] + "_" + now + ".json"
```

```
24    file = open(outputFile, 'a')
25    try:
26        tweets = Cursor(
27                        api.user_timeline,
28                        id=account['screen_name'],
29                        since_id=account['last_id'],
30                        wait_on_rate_limit=True,
31                        monitor_rate_limit=True,
32                        tweet_mode="extended"
33                      )
34        counter = 0
35        for tweet in tweets.items():
36            counter += 1
37            json.dump(tweet._json,file)
38            file.write("\n")
39            last_id = max(tweet.id,last_id)
40        conn = sqlite3.connect(timelineDB)
41        c = conn.cursor()
42        vals = (last_id,account['screen_name'])
43        c.execute("UPDATE accounts SET last_id=? WHERE screen_name=?", vals)
44        conn.commit()
45        conn.close()
46        log("Downloaded "+str(counter)+" new tweets from "+account['
      screen_name'])
47    except:
48        log("Error downloading tweets for account: "+account['screen_name'])
49    file.close()
```

Code Snippet 5.4 Advanced timeline downloader

This infrastructure means that instead of a one-time download of the timelines of several users, we can simply run this program regularly (perhaps even setting up your computer to automatically run it every day) and it will continuously download new tweets. An additional hidden functionality this gives us is that if we want to add a new screen name to start downloading, all we need to do is add it to the *accounts* table with a *last_id* of one, and then that account's timeline will be downloaded as far back as it will go, without redownloading anything we've already downloaded for the other accounts.

5.2.3 Additional User Data

In addition to the user's tweets, we can download a rich set of additional information about each user. Recall that in our setup of the database, we had a number of additional fields of interest for each user. These fields are included in the user object of the JSON with every single tweet that you download, or you can download this information separately on a per user basis. In Snippet 5.5, we show with file *snag_user.py* how to grab some additional fields of interest for all the accounts in our database. Lines 2 through 9 connect to the database and select all of the screen names in our database, while lines 12 through 14 set up our now familiar connection to the Twitter API.

For each screen name, we then connect to the API with the *get_user* method on line 19, and then save a set of the fields we get back from the JSON. However, we wrap this inside of a try/except statement in order to make sure that if there is a problem with getting the data for a particular user, our entire program doesn't crash. When a user deletes their account (or Twitter suspends their account), this method will throw an error. If that occurs, we print out the screen name that caused a problem along with the error message on line 21. We then set a dichotomous variable called *successful_download* so that we don't try to update the database if we were not able to get data for that screen name.

```
1  # Variable definitions
2  timelineDB = "data/timeline.db"
3
4  # Grab list of screen names to download
5  screen_names = []
6  conn = sqlite3.connect(timelineDB)
7  c = conn.cursor()
8  for r in c.execute("SELECT screen_name FROM accounts"):
9      screen_names.append(r[0])
10
11  # Connect to API
12  auth_handler = OAuthHandler(consumer_key,consumer_secret)
13  auth_handler.set_access_token(access_token,access_token_secret)
14  api = API(auth_handler)
15
16  for screen_name in screen_names:
17      successful_download=True
18      try:
19          u = api.get_user(screen_name, wait_on_rate_limit=True)
20      except Exception as e:
21          log(screen_name+": "+str(e))
22          successful_download=False
23
24      if successful_download:
25          q = (u.id,u.name,u.followers_count,u.friends_count,
26               u.statuses_count,u.verified,screen_name)
27          c.execute("""UPDATE accounts SET user_id=?,
28                       name=?,follower_count=?,friend_count=?,
29                       status_count=?,verified=?
30                       WHERE screen_name=?""", q)
31          conn.commit()
32
33  conn.close()
```

Code Snippet 5.5 Snagging additional information about users

The Twitter API reference has a full list of the fields available in the user object (including additional items like the URL of the user's profile picture). In this case, we are extracting some of the most used additional fields: the user's name, number of followers, number of friends, number of posted statuses, and whether the user is verified or not (i.e. has a blue checkmark). In addition, keep in mind that all of these values can change over time, and with some rapidity in the case of counts of statuses, followers, and friends. As such, if the quantity of interest is whether such components change over time, you can modify this code to keep a time-stamped record of what the values were at particular points in time.

5.2.4 Sample Project: Tracking Congress

Section 5.2.3 sets up the basic infrastructure for tracking any number of Twitter accounts, but in order to do network analysis we need data on a much larger set of users – in order to have sufficient nodes in order to build a proper network in the first place. Next we will set up an example project with a much larger base of data that we will use as the primary example for the rest of the chapter: the set of all the Twitter accounts of members of the 2018–2020 American Congress. This has the advantage of being a large enough set of data (535 individual users, with some 900 distinct Twitter handles) to build a complex network for analysis, but still small and defined enough to easily download en masse.

Figure 5.1 shows the first few lines of a CSV file (*congress.csv* in the sample code) that has several columns of data about each Twitter handle used by a member of Congress for the 2018–2020 session of Congress. The *user_id* and *screen_name* fields are the most important for our purposes since they allow us to scrape Twitter data, but the other fields are typically of substantive interest for research questions involving these accounts. This includes their party, state they serve, and the ICPSR number, which is a unique identifier for each individual who has ever served in Congress. Note that some of the individuals are repeated since they have multiple Twitter accounts.

	A	B	C	D	E	F	G	H
1	user_id	screen_name	party	chamber	state	bioname	icpsr	num_tweets
2	2962891515	RepAbraham	Republican	House	LA	ABRAHAM, Ralph	21522	366
3	1609364557	AlmaforCongress	Democrat	House	NC	ADAMS, Alma	21545	334
4	2916086925	RepAdams	Democrat	House	NC	ADAMS, Alma	21545	2315
5	76452765	Robert_Aderholt	Republican	House	AL	ADERHOLT, Robert	29701	475
6	41533245	aguilarpete	Democrat	House	CA	AGUILAR, Peter Rey	21506	1
7	21669223	LamarAlexander	Republican	Senate	TN	ALEXANDER, Lamar	40304	26
8	76649729	SenAlexander	Republican	Senate	TN	ALEXANDER, Lamar	40304	2078
9	385111151	rickallen	Republican	House	GA	ALLEN, Rick W.	21516	39
10	2964287128	RepRickAllen	Republican	House	GA	ALLEN, Rick W.	21516	465
11	346964561	ColinAllredTX	Democrat	House	TX	ALLRED, Colin	21900	431

Figure 5.1 Excerpt of CSV file containing congressional Twitter handles

Snippet 5.6 shows the modification of our database in *import_congress.py* to have a new table called *congress* with all of the fields we were previously tracking for accounts in addition to new fields from the new CSV file. Note that since everything about this new table is consistent with how we set up our previous infrastructure, all of our previous code downloading tweets (Snippet 5.4) and grabbing user details (Snippet 5.5) can be easily modified to point at this table instead of *accounts.csv* as we did in Snippet 5.3 and will otherwise work identically. Just downloading the tweets of this set of several hundred accounts will take several days of processing time, regardless of your available computing resources or bandwidth, simply because of the API's rate limitations on these queries.

```
1  # Variable definitions
2  inputFile = "congress.csv"
3  timelineDB = "data/timeline.db"
4
5  # Set up database structure
6  conn = sqlite3.connect(timelineDB)
7  c = conn.cursor()
8
9  # Set up a table for accounts
10 c.execute("""CREATE TABLE IF NOT EXISTS congress (
11              user_id BIGINT,
12              screen_name VARCHAR,
13              party VARCHAR,
14              icpsr VARCHAR,
15              chamber VARCHAR,
16              state VARCHAR,
17              last_id BIGINT,
18              name VARCHAR,
19              follower_count INT,
20              friend_count INT,
21              status_count INT,
22              verified INT
23          )""")
24 c.execute('''CREATE UNIQUE INDEX IF NOT EXISTS
25              idx_screen_name ON accounts(screen_name)''')
26
27 df = pd.read_csv(inputFile, encoding='UTF-8')
28
29 for index, row in df.iterrows():
30     q=(row['user_id'], row['screen_name'], row['party'],
31         row['icpsr'], row['chamber'], row['state'])
32     c.execute("""REPLACE INTO congress
33                 (user_id,screen_name,party,icpsr,
34                 chamber,state,last_id)
35                 VALUES (?,?,?,?,?,?,1)""", q)
36
37 conn.commit()
38 conn.close()
```

Code Snippet 5.6 Setting up database for downloading congressional timelines

5.3 Networks of Friends and Followers

Now that we have constructed infrastructure for collecting the data of individual Twitter users en masse, we can turn to building networks out of this data. In this section we will construct two types of networks based on the followers of the users we are tracking: a friends network and a cofriends network. To support this, in Snippet 5.7 we show the file *create_db_followers.py* and set up a database table for tracking the followers of users. The table has just two fields, both of which will contain unique ids of Twitter users: *user_id* indicates a particular user, and *followed_by* will contain the id of a user following the first user. In this way, we can track who follows whom on a database level.

```python
1  # Variable definitions
2  networkDB = "data/network.db"
3
4  # Set up database structure
5  conn = sqlite3.connect(networkDB)
6  c = conn.cursor()
7
8  # Set up a table for followers
9  c.execute("""CREATE TABLE IF NOT EXISTS followers (
10              user_id BIGINT,
11              followed_by BIGINT
12              )""")
13 c.execute('''CREATE UNIQUE INDEX IF NOT EXISTS
14              idx_followers ON followers(user_id,followed_by)''')
15
16 conn.commit()
17 conn.close()
```

Code Snippet 5.7 Setting up friend/follower database

Populating this table can be done from two different directions: we can either take a given user account and download a list of all the users they follow (dubbed "friends" in the Twitter API), or a list of all users that follow them. The former tends to be easier to collect because even if millions of people follow a certain account, that account will still follow a relatively limited number of other accounts. For example, the average member of Congress has 210 000 followers, but only 2 800 friends. Many Twitter accounts of extremely high-profile figures only follow a handful of accounts. For instance, Vladimir Putin's official English-language Twitter account has as of the summer of 2020 over 800 000 followers, but only follows 22 other accounts (notably including Barack Obama, but *not* Donald Trump).

While the Twitter API supports downloading a list of either the followers or friends of a particular account, it is rate-limited to only downloading 5 000 such ids at a time. This is more than the number of friends for almost all accounts, but pales in comparison to follower counts that can be in the millions for popular accounts. Snippet 5.8 shows the file *snag_friends.py* and demonstrates how to download all of the friends of a set of accounts using our infrastructure. Lines 5 through 9 grab all of the accounts we are tracking, and then connect to the Twitter API on lines 11 through 13 before looping through all the accounts. As with the *snag_user* code earlier in the chapter, we wrap the call to the API in a try/except statement so that if the screen name no longer exists the error is appropriately handled.

The key bit of code is line 20, which connects to the *friend_ids* component of the API and asks for all the unique ids of the accounts followed by the account in question. It does so using a cursor, which is effectively a way of paginating through sets of results when the total number is larger than the rate limit. Finally, it then saves each user-follower combination of user ids to our database in lines 30 and 31.

```
1  # Variable definitions
2  tweetsDB = "data/network.db"
3  accounts = []
4
5  conn = sqlite3.connect(tweetsDB)
6  c = conn.cursor()
7  for r in c.execute("SELECT user_id, screen_name FROM congress where user_id
       not in (select distinct followed_by from followers)"):
8      accounts.append({'user_id':r[0],
9                       'screen_name':r[1]})
10
11 auth_handler = OAuthHandler(consumer_key,consumer_secret)
12 auth_handler.set_access_token(access_token,access_token_secret)
13 api = API(auth_handler, wait_on_rate_limit=True)
14
15 for a in accounts:
16     log("getting: "+a['screen_name'])
17     friends = []
18     successful_download = True
19     try:
20         tc = tweepy.Cursor(api.friends_ids,screen_name=a['screen_name'])
21         for friend_id in tc.items():
22             friends.append(friend_id)
23     except Exception as e:
24         log(a['screen_name'] + ": " + str(e))
25         successful_download = False
26
27     if successful_download:
```

```
28      for friend_id in friends:
29          q=(friend_id,a['user_id'])
30          c.execute("""REPLACE INTO followers (user_id,followed_by)
31                  VALUES (?,?)""",q)
32      conn.commit()
33  conn.close()
```

Code Snippet 5.8 Downloading all friends of a set of accounts

The code will automatically pause and wait until your account's rate limit has been reset in cases where the amount you are grabbing exceeds that amount, which generally means it will sit idle for about 15 minutes waiting for reset to occur. It should take approximately 15 hours to download all of the friend ids for all members of Congress in this example, so when you run it, just set it to run overnight.

5.3.1 Friend Networks

Now that we have all of the friends of our set of accounts, we will create two different types of networks. First, let's create a friends network, which simply represents each of the accounts as nodes, and whether the accounts follow each other as the edges of the network. To do this, we will use a Python library called *networkx*, which contains support for an extensive array of network analysis. This type of network is called a *Directed Graph* because each of the edges between a pair of nodes has two components: from node A to node B and from node B to node A. The relevance to this example is that knowing whether (for example) Sam follows John is independent of whether John follows Sam.

Snippet 5.9 shows this in action from *generate_friends.py*. It imports our new network library on line 2, and then instantiates our network graph on line 5. The *DiGraph()* method creates a directed graph, while if we wanted a nondirected graph (with just one directionless edge between each pair of nodes) we'd use the more basic *Graph()* method (which we will use in the next example application). On line 9 we loop through all of the accounts in our database, and for each one create a node in our network on line 10. Note that the first value (the *user_id* in this case) is the unique name we want to give the node, while we can then define any additional further fields of interest by just naming them and assigning values to them. This can be a valuable tool when in more complicated applications we want to use attributes of the nodes (e.g. gender, political party, total number of tweets, etc.) in our network analysis.

```
 1 # Variable definitions
 2 import networkx as nx
 3 tweetsDB = "data/network.db"
 4
 5 G = nx.DiGraph()
 6
 7 conn = sqlite3.connect(tweetsDB)
 8 c = conn.cursor()
 9 for r in c.execute("SELECT user_id, screen_name, party FROM congress"):
10     G.add_node(r[0],screen_name=r[1])
11
12 for r in c.execute("""SELECT followed_by, user_id FROM followers WHERE
13                       user_id in (select user_id from congress) and
14                       followed_by in (select user_id from congress)"""):
15     G.add_edge(r[0],r[1])
16
17 conn.close()
```

Code Snippet 5.9 Generating a friends network

Next, on lines 12 through 15, we select from the followers table of our database all of the user-follower pairs in which both accounts are members of our list of accounts. That is, we are in this application *only* interested in the following behavior internal to our list of accounts. We then on line 15 add an edge (a connection) going *from* the following account *to* the followed account. The end result is a network that can be used with any of the standard network analysis tools that we discuss later in the chapter.

5.3.2 Co-friend Networks

Cofriend networks are networks in which the nodes are accounts and the edges are defined by the total number of friends the two accounts have in common. This is an undirected network (since there is just one edge between nodes) with weighted edges (since the edges are assigned a weight based on common friends rather than simply being dichotomous as in the previous example). Snippet 5.10 shows the file *generate_cofriend.py*, which generates this network from our congressional friends data. In line 5 it sets up an empty undirected network, and then on lines 8 through 10 creates a node for each congressional account in our database. Note that on line 10 when we set up the node, we do so with an empty *set* (an object that functions as a list that only contains unique items) called "friends" that we will use to store all the user ids that this node follows. Lines 12 through 15 loop through each of the congressional accounts, and select all the friends of each account, appending each user id to the friends list for the appropriate node on line 15.

```
1  # Variable definitions
2  import networkx as nx
3  tweetsDB = "data/network.db"
4
5  G = nx.Graph()
6
7  conn = sqlite3.connect(tweetsDB)
8  c = conn.cursor()
9  for r in c.execute("SELECT user_id, screen_name, party FROM congress"):
10     G.add_node(r[0], screen_name=r[1], friends=set())
11
12 for n in G.nodes():
13     for r in c.execute("""SELECT user_id FROM followers
14                         WHERE followed_by=?""",[n]):
15         G.nodes[n]['friends'].add(r[0])
16
17 for a in G.nodes():
18     log("(Building network): " + G.nodes[a]['screen_name'])
19     for b in G.nodes():
20         if a!=b:
21             common = len(G.nodes[a]['friends'] & G.nodes[b]['friends'])
22             G.add_edge(a,b,weight=common)
23
24 conn.close()
```

Code Snippet 5.10 Generating a Co-friends network

At this point in the code, we have all of our nodes created and for each node have a list of the ids that it follows. What we need to do is calculate how many of the friends overlap for each pair of nodes. We do this by having a nested loop in which we iterate over all of the nodes twice, which we do on lines 17 through 22, with the outer loop designated as *a* and the inner loop *b*. We use the "&" operator for sets on line 21, which just returns an array of the items that appear on *both* sets a and b. By taking the length of that array, we have the total number of user ids that appear on the friends lists of both nodes. We then create an edge between a and b on line 22, with the weight of the edge being set to that number. Also note that in line 20 we skip this creation of an edge if a and b are the same node.

With very small modifications, we could adapt this code to create a similar network for any other weighted counts of comparable social media behavior among users. For example, instead of compiling a list of friends, we could instead compile a list of all distinct hashtags in each user's tweet history using the entity extraction code from Chapter 5. Snippet 5.11 shows the file *generate_cohashtag.py* as an example of this technique. Note that it functions *exactly* the same as the cofriend network generator above except that it renames the array in question *hashtags* instead of *friends* and on lines 13 to 15 selects the distinct hashtags used by each user instead of the user ids of their followers. The end result is a network with user accounts as nodes, and edges being the number of hashtags *both* users used in their tweets.

```
1   # Variable definitions
2   import networkx as nx
3   tweetsDB = "data/network.db"
4
5   G = nx.Graph()
6
7   conn = sqlite3.connect(tweetsDB)
8   c = conn.cursor()
9   for r in c.execute("SELECT user_id, screen_name FROM accounts"):
10      G.add_node(r[0],screen_name=r[1],hashtags=set())
11
12  for n in G.nodes():
13      for r in c.execute("""SELECT distinct(hashtag) FROM hashtags
14                          WHERE tweet_id IN
15                          (SELECT id FROM tweets WHERE user_id=?)""",[n]):
16          G.nodes[n]['hashtags'].add(r[0])
17
18  for a in G.nodes():
19      log("(Building network): " + G.nodes[a]['screen_name'])
20      for b in G.nodes():
21          if a!=b:
22              common = len(G.nodes[a]['hashtags'] & G.nodes[b]['hashtags'])
23              G.add_edge(a,b,weight=common)
24
25  conn.close()
```

Code Snippet 5.11 Generating a Co-hashtags network

A similar tweak could be done to incorporate any of the entities extracted in Chapter 3. Thus we could create networks of the hashtags, images, videos, mentions, or URLs that users have in common in their tweets. Retweet networks are a popular subset of this type of network, in which the weighted edges are the number of retweets the two nodes have in common. Alternately, one can create multidimensional networks in which multiple edges are defined between each node, in order to accommodate *all* of these entities in the same network structure.

5.3.3 Networks with Entities as Nodes

An additional approach is to invert networks so that rather than the nodes being users, they are entities such as hashtags. In this case, the edges are weighted by the number of times the two hashtags appeared in the same tweet. This sort of network has applications related to content analysis in which our substantive questions revolve around what sorts of content coexists with each other within the same posted tweets. Snippet 5.12 shows the file *generate_hashtag.py*, which constructs this sort of network.

```
1  # Variable definitions
2  import networkx as nx
3  tweetsDB = "data/network.db"
4
5  G = nx.Graph()
6
7  conn = sqlite3.connect(tweetsDB)
8  c = conn.cursor()
9  for r in c.execute("""SELECT hashtag,count(*) FROM hashtags
10                        GROUP BY hashtag ORDER BY count(*) DESC
11                        LIMIT 100"""):
12     G.add_node(r[0],tweets=set())
13
14 for n in G.nodes():
15     for r in c.execute("""SELECT tweet_id FROM hashtags
16                           WHERE hashtag=?""",[n]):
17         G.nodes[n]['tweets'].add(r[0])
18
19 for a in G.nodes():
20     for b in G.nodes():
21         if a!=b:
22             common = len(G.nodes[a]['tweets'] & G.nodes[b]['tweets'])
23             G.add_edge(a,b,weight=common)
24
25 conn.close()
```

Code Snippet 5.12 Generating a hashtag network

Note that it is a modification of the networks in Section 5.3.2, with the same basic logic as a cofriend network that defined users as nodes. In this case, in lines 9 to 11 when setting up the nodes, we instead select the hundred most commonly used hashtags from our hashtags table. We are only restricting this in order to eliminate the vast long tail of hashtags used only in a handful of tweets in order to make our network more tractable for analysis. In addition, we figure the weighting by comparing the number of tweet ids that are in common between any two nodes. One could modify this to instead use any other entity (such as images or videos) as the fundamental node of the network.

5.4 Basics of Network Analysis

Having created a variety of different networks, we can now turn to some basic network analysis. One of the basic tools in the network analysis toolkit is calculating centrality for the nodes of the network. Centrality is a catchall term for various measures of how each individual node is situated in and interacts with the rest of the network. Depending on the research project, a number of different centralities may be appropriate, in order to operationalize different concepts. Note that different measures of centrality are not necessarily correlated with each other at all, as they measure different network attributes.

Three of the most commonly used forms of centrality are degree centrality, closeness centrality, and betweenness centrality. *Degree* centrality is the total number of edges that a particular node has, i.e. the number of links to other nodes. This can be useful for operationalizing how well-connected specific users are in the pool of users that you are monitoring. *Closeness* centrality is the average number of edges it takes for a node to connect to every other node in the network. *Betweenness* centrality measures how important each node is in creating bridges between other nodes. It does so by calculating the shortest path between every pair of nodes in the network, and then determining the proportion of those shortest paths that pass through each node in question.

To calculate these for the nodes in the networks we have created, we first need to set up our database so as to store the calculate values. In our examples in this section, we will use the friends network of members of Congress we built in the last section. As such, in Snippet 5.13 we modify the table that has the congressional Twitter handles so that we also have columns for the three basic types of centrality.

```
1  networkDB = "data/network.db"
2
3  # Set up database structure
4  conn = sqlite3.connect(networkDB)
5  c = conn.cursor()
6
7  c.execute("ALTER TABLE congress ADD centrality_degree FLOAT")
8  c.execute("ALTER TABLE congress ADD centrality_closeness FLOAT")
9  c.execute("ALTER TABLE congress ADD centrality_betweenness FLOAT")
10
11 conn.commit()
12 conn.close()
```

Code Snippet 5.13 Modifying database for calculating centrality

Next, we use built in tools from the NetworkX library to calculate each of these centralities. We do so with the file *centrality.py* as shown in Snippet 5.14 by first generating the directional graph on lines 5 through 15 as we did in Snippet 5.9. Next, on line 17, we calculate the degree centrality of every node using the *degree_centrality* function, and then loop over these centralities and save them to our database on lines 18–21. We then repeat the process two more times for closeness and betweenness centrality. The end result will be that the Congress table in our database will have each of the three centralities for each account stored with that account.

```python
1  # Variable definitions
2  import networkx as nx
3  tweetsDB = "data/network.db"
4
5  G = nx.DiGraph()
6
7  conn = sqlite3.connect(tweetsDB)
8  c = conn.cursor()
9  for r in c.execute("SELECT user_id, screen_name, party FROM congress"):
10     G.add_node(r[0],screen_name=r[1],party=r[2])
11
12 for r in c.execute("""SELECT followed_by, user_id FROM followers WHERE
13                       user_id in (select user_id from congress) and
14                       followed_by in (select user_id from congress)"""):
15     G.add_edge(r[0],r[1])
16
17 centralities = nx.degree_centrality(G)
18 for user_id in centralities:
19     q = (centralities[user_id],user_id)
20     c.execute("""UPDATE congress SET centrality_degree=?
21                  WHERE user_id=?""",q)
22
23 centralities = nx.closeness_centrality(G)
24 for user_id in centralities:
25     q = (centralities[user_id],user_id)
26     c.execute("""UPDATE congress SET centrality_closeness=?
27                  WHERE user_id=?""",q)
28
29 centralities = nx.betweenness_centrality(G)
30 for user_id in centralities:
31     q = (centralities[user_id],user_id)
32     c.execute("""UPDATE congress SET centrality_betweenness=?
33                  WHERE user_id=?""",q)
34
35 conn.commit()
36 conn.close()
```

Code Snippet 5.14 Calculating and saving centrality of nodes

There are a plethora of network analysis techniques available both in the existing Python network libraries and in external software such as R and Gephi. The latter is a graphical interface that is especially useful for generating meaningful visualizations of network data, in addition to tools such as community detection. As such, we will often want to use our Python infrastructure to generate the

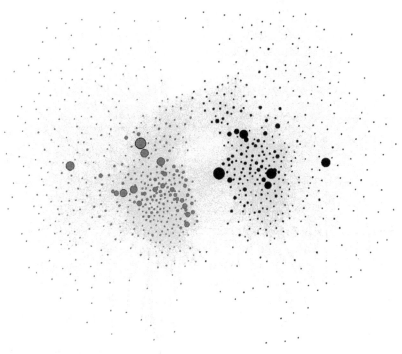

Figure 5.2 Visualizing social media networks: a congressional friends network

basics of our networks from our social media data, and then export that network for use in other software.

For example, Figure 5.2 shows an example of using Gephi to render our congressional friends network, with the nodes representing congressional Twitter accounts, and the edges representing whether they both follow each other. In this example, the size of the node has been made proportional to the betweenness centrality of each node (so that more central nodes are larger), while the color represents political party (black for Republican, gray for Democrat).

Snippet 5.15 shows how to take any of our existing networks and export them in two ways. First, line 1 shows how to write a network object to an external *.gexf* file, which is a file specially formatted for importation into Gephi. It contains all information about nodes and edges necessary for additional analysis and visualization. Second, lines 2 and 3 show how to take a network and reformat it into an adjacency matrix that is then saved to a CSV file. Adjacency matrices are similar to correlation matrices in that the set of all nodes is used to make both rows and columns, so that any given cell is the relationship (i.e. the edge) between any given pair of nodes. This file can be directly imported into R in order to make use of its network analysis libraries.

```
1  nx.write_gexf(G, 'congress.gexf')
2  adjacency = nx.to_pandas_adjacency(G)
3  adjacency.to_csv('congress_adj.csv', index=False)
```

Code Snippet 5.15 Exporting network data from Python

5.5 Solving the Bot Problem

Bots are one of the most commonly raised concerns with any usage of social media data in scientific work. After all, how can we trust measurements obtained of tweets and user behavior if it turns out that large proportions of the activity we are measuring is the result not of individuals posting in good faith, but of automated accounts producing fake content? This is particularly salient for social scientific work where the concepts we are studying are very often the ones that malicious actors are intentionally trying to influence through bot activity. Social media companies are engaged behind the scenes in a constant effort of weeding out and deleting bot accounts of this nature (though their efficacy and root motivations are hotly debated). Twitter has released several large datasets for researchers that contain all user accounts (along with their full sets of tweets) removed as part of different waves of bot activity (such as bots engaged in the 2016 American presidential campaign). These datasets are publicly available through Twitter's website, and are stored in the same JSON format that we use throughout this book, so they are usable with the tools that we have built.

One of the cornerstones of bot detection algorithms is network analysis, because the friend and follower networks of bots tend to be very distinct compared to real users. Early algorithms took advantage of the fact that bots tended to be accounts with no friends or followers, and later only had self-contained friend networks. That is, all the bots' followers were *other* bots in the same network of bots in order to at face value mimic the follower count of a real user. Detecting bots is an ever-evolving set of tools as detection schemes become more sophisticated, and designers of bots adapt to work around the newest detection algorithms.

It is essential for social media researchers to be able to incorporate bot detection in their work, as even in otherwise unrelated work, it can be important for robustness and validity checks to evaluate whether results are being driven by bot activity rather than genuine activity by human beings. However, since bot detection is always evolving as bots themselves become more sophisticated, I recommend using an off-the-shelf solution to bot detection rather than programming it oneself from scratch. This has the advantage of being specialized software working at the cutting edge of bot detection, kept up to date by researchers specializing in those techniques. Using bot detection frameworks provided by academic sources ensures that the necessities of transparency and rigor are maintained. While writing bot detection from scratch is beyond the scope of this book we can write code to tap into existing bot detection algorithms with access provided via an API. In particular, we will implement bot detection by connecting to the Botometer tool developed by researchers at Indiana University (Yang et al., 2019). In order to use this tool, you will need to register for an account at RapidAPI, the site through which the API is provided. This does not cost anything (although you can pay if you want to process more data than is allowed by the usual Twitter API restrictions) but will provide you with an API key (a long alphanumeric string) that you need to add to the *my_settings.py* file in our codebase (set up in Section 2.4.2) on line 17 (labeled *botometer_key*), similarly to how at the beginning of this book you entered key values for the Twitter API. Once you do so, the rest of the code in this section will work.

The basic way that the Botometer API works is for you to provide it a Twitter user id, and it will return a JSON object that contains a variety of metrics about that user's probability of being an automated account. It does so both in a language-neutral manner (relying strictly on user attributes and network analysis) and also by supplementing that with content analysis of the user's tweets (which is valid only for English-language content). As such, we create a new table in our database called *bot_users* in Snippet 5.16 that contains the id of each user, in addition to numerical fields called *bot_english* and *bot_universal* that will contain these two probabilities.

```
1  import sqlite3
2
3  conn = sqlite3.connect("data/tweets.db")
4  c = conn.cursor()
5  c.execute('''CREATE TABLE bot_users (
6               user_id BIGINT,
7               bot_english FLOAT,
8               bot_universal FLOAT
9               )''')
10
11 c.execute('''CREATE UNIQUE INDEX bot_idx_id ON bot_users(user_id)''')
12
13 conn.commit()
14 conn.close()
```

Code Snippet 5.16 Modifying database for storing bot probability

Next, in Snippet 5.17 we show the file *detect_bots.py*. It connects to Botometer on lines 5 through 7 using a method intentionally designed to be very similar to the connections to the Twitter API that we have used repeatedly. It then connects to our database on lines 9 through 13, and loops through all of the distinct users in a table of tweets. It then loops through each of those accounts and queries the Botometer API for its analysis of that account on line 15. Line 16 checks to make sure there is actually something to save to our database (if the user account has been deleted or is not accessible for some other reason, there will be no "scores" element of the JSON response) and then inserts that account's results into our new table.

```
1  # Variable definitions
2  import botometer
3  tweetsDB = "data/tweets.db"
4
5  bom = botometer.Botometer(wait_on_ratelimit=True,
6                            mashape_key=botometer_key,
7                            **twitter_app_auth)
8
9  accounts = []
10 conn = sqlite3.connect(tweetsDB)
11 c = conn.cursor()
12 for r in c.execute("SELECT distinct user_id FROM tweets"):
13     accounts.append(r[0])
14
15 for id, result in bom.check_accounts_in(accounts):
16     if 'scores' in result:
17         q = (id, result['scores']['english'],
18                  result['scores']['universal'])
19         c.execute("""REPLACE INTO bot_users
20                      (user_id,bot_english,bot_universal)
21                      VALUES (?,?,?)""", q)
22         conn.commit()
23 c.close()
```

Code Snippet 5.17 Using botometer to estimate bot probability

Note that this could equally be used on *any* of our collections of tweets that we have collected at any point in this book. Or it could be easily modified to analyze a predetermined set of accounts. Since the Botometer API is at its root limited by the same rate limits as the Twitter API (because underneath the hood, it connects to that API to get the activity and friend networks of these users), it can only handle 180 accounts per 15 minutes. As such, you may want to limit the number of accounts you query, or take a predetermined random sample of your overall body of users. Doing so can give you an idea of the proportion of activity in your corpus of tweets that appears to be from bots, or at least is above a certain probability threshold.

It is important to realize that the results of bot detection do not necessarily have an absolute objective meaning. For instance, establishing that 10% of the users in your database are above a 95% probability of being automated accounts does not inherently mean anything as a large or small quantity. These results are most useful in a comparative context. For instance, if that figure is substantially higher among accounts posting about your particular topic of substantive interest than it is in a random sample of social media activity, that may be significant to note.

In addition, this tool can be used in conjunction with other analytic techniques in this book in order to capture additional information. For instance, if you are testing hypotheses regarding bot activity, contrasting topic models of likely bot accounts in your sample with topic models of the content from nonbot accounts.

5.6 Key Takeaways

In this chapter, we have covered how to create your own infrastructure for monitoring the timelines of specific users, in addition to developing the tools necessary for building a variety of network structures for analysis using the particulars of social media data. Finally, we developed the basics of using network analysis on our social media data including the important application of detecting bot activity in your collected data.

6　The Ethics of Using Social Media Data

This chapter covers the particular ethical concerns raised by using social media data. This includes concerns frequently raised by IRBs in terms of human subjects research, and some of the thorny issues raised by the terms of use of social media sites with regard to data sharing and replicability. It will walk through what scholars need to know about the limitations imposed by Twitter's terms of use, what use cases are considered acceptable use (sharing data among researchers on the same project), and strategies for common scholarly needs that fall within gray areas (for example, providing lists of tweet ids so that a dataset can be fully replicated, but the terms of use conditions regarding republication of tweets are not violated). In addition, it covers issues of researcher trauma, with regard to the risk of exposure to explicit and violent content through social media. Finally, it concludes with the personal experience of the author in approaching these ethical conundrums in good faith.

6.1　Social Media and the IRB

Institutional review boards (IRBs) are intended to provide oversight over research that is performed on human subjects. In response to now famously abusive cases of experimentation, the Belmont Report was commissioned in 1976 in order to create a framework for ethics in human research (National Commission for the Protection of Human Subjects of Biomedical and Behavioral Research, 1978). The Report established three essential principles:

1. *Respect:* Treat people with respect, obtain informed consent, and be truthful.
2. *Beneficence:* Do no harm to the research subjects, maximize benefits for the research project while minimizing risk to participants.
3. *Justice:* Distribute the costs and benefits of research to the subjects equally and fairly.

These principles formed the basis of the IRB's Common Rule, which went into effect for the first time in 1991 and governs approval or disapproval of human subjects research in academia (Tene and Polonetsky, 2015). While the ethical foundation of the Common Rule remained sound, the details of implementation were wholly inadequate to the eventual implications of social media.

Social media research is not performed at the human scale at which the Belmont principles were formulated, and thus rules that made sense to govern researching individuals one-by-one failed to adapt to research done on thousands or millions of individuals in aggregate (Bailey, Dittrich, and Kenneally, 2013). This is most clear in the case of early social media research being stymied by IRBs applying the informed consent rules to large-scale data collection. The first time I applied for an NSF (National Science Foundation) grant to set up a large-scale social media downloader, my application was rejected by the University's IRB out of hand, with the explanation that it was only permissible to read the tweets of individuals from whom I first received written consent.

The utter infeasibility of such a requirement is obvious, but infeasibility in and of itself isn't an exemption from ethics. But there are two elements to social media data that make such restrictions not in the spirit of the original Belmont Report.

First, social media data is at least implicitly public. While someone who posts a tweet has not signed a consent form authorizing the use of that tweet for a specific research project, there is an intuitive notion that by posting something publicly, they are offering it so that others might read it, interpret it, or, indeed, research it. This isn't legalistic hairsplitting to get research design approval, but goes to the heart of how social media has fundamentally changed society and communication.

Two generations ago, only powerful actors and institutions had the capacity to make public statements in the sense that the rest of the world could potentially and freely read it. The genius of social media is that rather than communication being restricted to elite actors who owned the means of transmission such as printing presses and television transmitters, now everyone has the capacity to transmit (Wilson, 2016). Requiring individual signed consent to research social media posts is as absurd as requiring the signed consent of newspaper publishers in order to read their articles for research. The United Nations Declaration of Human Rights asserts every individual's "right to science," which includes the right to *participate* in science, and as such the public posting of normal individuals should be held as usable in scientific research as those of elites (Vayena et al., 2016; Vayena and Tasioulas, 2016).

Second, social media data is, generally speaking, on the correct side of the Belmont Report's second principle, in that the collection of publicly available data en masse represents minimal risk to the human subjects being researched. As Halavais argued in 2011, while change was still on the horizon, conservative IRBs were regularly treating nonintrusive and anonymized data collection as functionally equivalent to human experimentation (Halavais, 2011).

I say *generally* because there are examples of social media data collection that have clearly violated the second principle. For instance, consider the now notorious 2008 study of Facebook "Tastes, Ties, Time," in which a specific college cohort's Facebook postings and metadata were scraped for years, including ethnicities, college majors, state of origin, and other personal data (Lewis et al., 2008). Although the data was anonymized before publication, the idiosyncrasies of the data (size of the graduating class, number of individuals with rare ethnicities, frequencies of majors) allowed it to be deanonymized within days of publication (Zimmer, 2010). Even when researchers follow best practices of anonymization of data, it has been repeatedly shown that when unrelated public datasets are merged together such that data points useless on their own can be combined together algorithmically, deanonymization is still possible (Lazer et al., 2021).

The combination of overly restrictive IRBs and the Wild West mentality of early researchers making their own rules was not tenable in the long run. The Association of Internet Researchers took the lead with producing well-considered sets of ethics guidelines in an evolving document in the early 2000s (the most recent version was made available in 2020) (Franzke et al., 2020; Markham and Buchanan, 2012). The Department of Homeland Security produced a document called the Menlo Report in 2012, which updated the Belmont Report so that its principles "can be usefully applied in fields related to research about or involving information and communication technology" (Bailey et al., 2012). This culminated in revisions to the Common Rule itself, beginning with the Secretary's Advisory Committee on Human Research Protections producing a set of recommendations in 2013 that were long debated before final revisions to the Common Rule went into effect in 2018 (Secretary's Advisory Committee on Human Research Protections, 2013).

The primary change relevant to social media research is that the Common Rule now does not consider social media data to meet the definition of human subjects research unless the information is obtained through intervention or includes information that is both identifiable *and* private. Strictly observational social media data meets the former by definition, and meets the latter in most instances. The official guidance on the Common Rule, published by a joint document of the Department of Health and Human Services and National Institutes of Health, states that:

> Essentially, if the content can be accessed by any Internet user without specific permission or authorization being required from the individual who posted the information or from the entity controlling access to the information, the post is considered "public" and therefore does not meet the "identifiable private information" criteria for human subjects research (HCIRB/BRP/DC-CPS, 2019).

The document specifically cites the example of analyzing YouTube videos, as something that may contain identifiable information, but is not considered private.

It is important to emphasize though that this exemption is explicitly provided for observational social media data, that is, social media data collected without a researcher intervention. While this book has focused exclusively on observational data, there is a growing field of research introducing external interventions via social media and studying the effects of the "treatment." The techniques covered in this book can certainly be used to collect such data, even if the implementation of interventions themselves (like using bots to post responses to certain tweets of the public, for instance) are not covered. IRB approval needs to be sought under the human subjects umbrella the moment a researcher intervention is planned as part of research.

Interventions can provide valuable scientific data, and can be designed such that they follow the essential ethical maxim of doing no harm to the participants. A subgenre of research has emerged using the easy communication afforded by social media as a way to perform experiments on shifting individual's attitudes based on the message sent, and the perception of *who* sent the message. Some standout efforts have been using bots (with variance on the perceived race of the bot account) sanctioning users for racist social media behavior (Munger, 2017), sending messages from different social classes to encourage political reflection in Colombian social media discussion (Gallego et al., 2019), and sanctioning partisan incivility in American political discussion (Munger, 2021). What unifies projects like this is that expectation of the treatment effect is to have a net normatively positive impact, with no risk to the individuals receiving the treatment.

Further guidance is offered in terms of exactly how to fill out the IRB forms when applying for approval for a project like those discussed throughout this book. In particular it says to answer "no" to the question "are human subjects involved" where it appears on forms G.220 and G.500. However, the question "does the proposed research involve human specimens and/or data?" should be answered "yes," and a justification statement should be attached. That statement should describe the data being collected, including any identifying information (such as user name on the site), an explanation of how that data is publicly available, and a data protection plan describing "precautions to mitigate potential risks" (HCIRB/BRP/DCCPS, 2019).[1]

---

[1] Ethics boards outside the United States will of course have their own rules on the matter, which may be more conservative. For example, some scholars have chafed under some of the United Kingdom's particularly conservative research ethics committee rulings on social media data collection (Hibbin, Samuel, and Derrick, 2018).

While this revision opens the door to social media research, some scholars are dissatisfied, and their concerns should be kept in mind when designing research for IRB approval. Some feel that the revisions should have simply defined social media as a public space, excluding it from the IRB process entirely instead of allowing IRBs to grant exemptions for it (Dingwall, 2017). While the so-called IRB sledgehammer may prevent some abuse, it also stifles a variety of big-data work, which tends to be exploratory and unamenable to collecting the minimal data required for testing predefined hypotheses (Garfinkel, 2017; Naser, 2015).

Finally, the Health Communication and Informatics Research Branch (HCIRB)'s clarification that social media data as described above "would be considered public unless existing law or the privacy policies/terms of service of the entity hosting the information indicate otherwise" should also give researchers pause (HCIRB/BRP/DCCPS, 2019). While IRBs will typically give an exemption for observational data collection, responsibility for remaining within the terms of use of the target website still rests with the researcher (Clifton, 2015; Diesner and Chin, 2015; Dingwall, 2017).

This is a much more complicated proposition than it appears at face value. For instance, Twitter's terms of use for the Developer API forbids using it for "monitoring sensitive events (including but not limited to protests, rallies, or community organizing meetings)" (Twitter, 2018). Depending on one's interpretation of "monitoring," the hundreds of academic studies on the use of Twitter by protesters are in violation of the terms of use. In addition, it forbids "profiling individuals based on … political affiliation or beliefs, racial or ethnic origin, religious or philosophical affiliation or beliefs" (Twitter, 2018), which depending on the interpretation of "profiling" could essentially outlaw any use of Twitter data in almost any imaginable social science context. Since Twitter is fully aware of the thousands of researchers using this data for exactly these purposes, it is clear that *it* doesn't interpret this as a violation of its terms of use, whatever it might literally say. But that could change at any point if it became expedient to the corporation.

In addition, we are somewhat spoiled in the Western world by the notion that social media companies by and large believe that they are a force for good. They may do a terrible job of it, they may make ethically unsound decisions when the choice is between ethics and profit, and they may stumble into all the traps of naively believing that good engineering can solve problems with social and political roots. The fact that they are trying is not a defense for their failing, but it makes them categorically different than a host of other social media companies around the world, which present a different set of ethical challenges for researchers.

Take for instance VKontakte (VK), the Facebook clone that is enormously popular in the Russian-speaking world, with over 500 million users. The founder was forced out of control of the company, and subsequently fled Russia entirely as the company was taken over by a media conglomerate run by close allies of the Putin regime. This has effectively made VK part of the extended network of state media in Russia, albeit a *social* media company. The users of VK are – knowingly or not – turning their data over to agents of an authoritarian regime. Any data a researcher collects from VK is data that is already in the hands of a dictator, rather than being data that can be co-opted by a dictator. This makes the ethics of data collection a quagmire: What course of action best respects the principle of minimizing harm in such a situation? Does a researcher have an ethical obligation to follow the terms of use of such a site when collecting data? What if VK added a clause to its terms of use *requiring* that anyone discovering antiregime activity was required to report it to the Russian authorities? Similar ethical cases could easily arise in other authoritarian regimes like China, which runs its own domestic alternatives to popular social media platforms.

Finally, in more mundane terms, terms of use can cause complications with basic scientific requirements such as replicability of datasets. Twitter's terms of use forbid the wholesale reposting of content, which makes reposting complete replication datasets a violation of the terms of use. There are a couple of work-arounds of which to be aware. First, sharing full data *within* a research team has never in practice been considered a violation by Twitter. Second, posting of the unique identifier of tweets en masse is also not a violation of the terms of use, and so replication datasets of Twitter data hosted in Dataverse tend to simply be lists of tweet ids. Note that the very first Twitter data collector we built in this book was one that looped through a list of tweet ids and downloaded them. This allows researchers to provide some form of replicability without violating the terms of use.

6.2 Ethics in Web Scraping

As part of my dissertation, I collected a variety of data on the ways that software was downloaded or used in different countries around the world. This was part of a broader effort to measure the technical literacy of populations and regimes. That is, measuring the number of per capita downloads of different web servers and programming language compilers as one input to a factor analysis estimating the level of technical ability the population in each country had. I had identified SourceForge, which is a repository of the source code of thousands of open source projects, as an ideal source for collecting some of this data.

SourceForge had an application programming interface (API) that allowed code to query how many downloads a particular project had in a particular month, reporting the results by country, in a JSON format not dissimilar to the ones documented in this book. I therefore wrote a simple loop that downloaded the individual names of every project on SourceForge (a list hundreds of thousands long) and then pinged the SourceForge API for the number of downloads each of those projects had, in each and every month for the decade time frame of the project. After starting this process I went to bed and woke up the next morning to find that not only had my program catastrophically errored out many hours before, but that it now didn't work at all. Further, I couldn't even access SourceForge through a web browser anymore, just receiving an error message.

What had happened will be obvious to many programmers reading this, many of whom have similar stories from their past when they inadvertently did something similar. Web servers can only handle a certain number of requests for information. If too many people access a website at once, it will get overwhelmed and be unable to respond. When this is done maliciously (as when hackers tell millions of hacked computers to simultaneously try to access the same website) it is called a denial-of-service (DoS) attack.

This can also happen naturally when there are huge spikes in web traffic for legitimate reasons that overwhelm the planned-for capacity of a website. For instance, on the morning of 9/11, every news website on the Internet was unreachable because of the sheer numbers of people all trying to access them at once. That morning, ESPN.com (which at the time was one of the most trafficked sites on the Internet and capable of much higher levels of traffic) simply mirrored the content of various news sites in an admirable act of public good. To this day, movie ticket websites tend to become unusable when a new Marvel or Star Wars film has tickets first go on sale.

As such, because even normal behavior can cause catastrophic issues if it spikes in a bad way, web systems tend to have a lot of automatic controls for heading off problems before they cause an issue. Without any conscious human intervention, many sites will automatically ban an IP address for a time if it seems to be accessing the site in an unusual way, such as sending a new request as soon as the old one finishes, much faster than a human being actually could be clicking in such a manner in their web browser.

My project was effectively launching a DoS against SourceForge, making requests as fast as my network connection would allow. Their server, with its thousands of users and hundreds of thousands of projects, was likely unaffected in any meaningful way. But it nonetheless automatically banned my IP address because the behavior it was engaging in was nonstandard and much higher in bandwidth than the normal usage of a human being.

That is the key rule of thumb to use when building web-scraping systems of any sort: Don't set up a downloader that hits a web server harder than a human being could through a web browser. This isn't about not getting caught, but about acting in good faith. These sites have data that you want, so don't try to download it faster than they intend for it to be downloaded.

A good practice for handling this is to simply add a "sleep" statement in your code inside whatever loop governs jumping from page to page. In Python, the command "time.sleep(x)" will pause the code's execution for x number of seconds. An additional good practice is to randomize x between loops, for instance, have it be a random number of seconds between 10 and 30 seconds each loop. This further makes your system behave more like a human being in a web browser, and thus makes your activity even less disruptive to the web server itself.

Note of course that this can make the process of scraping a large quantity of data take an extraordinarily long time. One alternative is to contact the website in question in order to ask if they can provide the data you are seeking all in one batch. Mileage may vary on this front of course, large companies will likely be unwilling to, and may not even respond at all. However, a significant number of companies providing social media services in particular tend to view their work through a utopian lens, and as such can be surprisingly sympathetic to an appeal of charity toward science.

The rule of thumb does not apply when a site provides an API for you to access. In that case, the API will be throttled to the level that the site has decided it wants to support. So for instance, the Twitter streaming API is set up to allow downloading of millions of tweets per day (set to no more than 1% of all activity on Twitter from moment to moment). It is an extremely robust API that is difficult to push the limits of without intending to because of the sheer amount of hardware needed to do so.

6.3 Researcher Trauma

For the 2018 American midterm elections, a coauthor and I set up streaming data collection of a wide selection of keywords relevant to those elections. We had a number of potential projects in mind, one of which involved geographic variation in extremist and hate speech leading up to the election. My coauthor, the expert on American elections of the two of us, dove deeply down the rabbit hole of hate speech on Twitter. He searched for obvious racial slurs relevant to our research, read the timelines of people using those slurs, and took notes on the other language they used in order to create a rough dictionary of hate speech for the purposes of further data collection.

Needless to say, this wasn't a pleasant research experience. It was stressful and more than a little disturbing.

Social media's low barrier to entry for data collection, with little in the way of physical constraints, makes it easy for a researcher to be exposed to all manner of horrors in the course of all stages of a research project. This is exacerbated by the fact that the ease of data collection means there is no physical boundary that is crossed giving a psychological buffer to exposure. Rather than horror being at a mental arm's length, on the other end of a flight or a drive to somewhere else, the horror is at your fingertips. It is as close as checking your email or prepping slides for class.

The psychological effects of exposure to the suffering of others have been long recognized in the social sciences and have been studied under several different labels such as "vicarious trauma." Vicarious trauma's effects have been documented in repeated studies going back decades (Dickson-Swift et al., 2008; Figley, 1985, 1995, 2002; Pearlman and McKay, 2008; Pearlman and Saakvitne, 1995). Particular case studies have focused on a variety of fields of workers who are at risk for vicarious trauma: social workers, health workers, criminal lawyers, transcribers, probation officers, clergy, even veterinarians (Etherington, 2007; Figley and Roop, 2006; Nikischer, 2018). Vicarious trauma's effects have been classified as "secondary traumatic stress," which is "nearly identical to post-traumatic stress including symptoms associated with post-traumatic stress disorder (PTSD) such as intrusive imagery, avoidance, hyperarousal, distressing emotions, cognitive changes, and functional impairment" (Bride, Radey, and Figley, 2007, p. 156).

While this extensive literature largely focuses on workers rather than researchers, the same principles apply. Loyle and Simoni (2017) call this specifically "researcher trauma" and note that it "happens over time as a researcher witnesses and/or hears distressing stories, or deals with distressing data." Of particular relevance to the use of social media data, it has been found that "coding news articles and victim testimony can be as impactful as personally interviewing victims" (Loyle and Simoni, 2017, p. 142). Coding social media data falls into that same category, and can conceivably be even more impactful than newspaper coding because it is rawer and more direct, not filtered through a journalist's framing.

The fields where vicarious trauma was initially identified, such as social and health work, have an advantage in dealing with such trauma in that by being therapeutic, they offer a psychological compensation for the feelings of trauma. That is, "compassion fatigue" is balanced in some part by the "compassion satisfaction" of knowing that the work is helping the person whose pain you are witnessing (Woodby et al., 2011). Research projects, however, are about data collection, and while we may hope our work contributes to solving the problems we research in the long run, that is an abstract hope disconnected from the immediate experience of horror (Bride, Radey, and Figley, 2007, p. 156).

The nature of social media data as "big data" can reinforce feelings of futility. Whereas there is an end to recordings that need to be transcribed, newspaper articles that need to be coded, or victims who need to be interviewed, there are always more tweets than can ever be read. Staring into the abyss was never just a danger because of its darkness, but because of its infiniteness.

Exacerbating the potential trauma is that institutional recognition of the problem is often lacking. While most of what we know about vicarious trauma is from efforts to remedy it in fields like health and social work, "outside of these fields, there is often a complete lack of understanding that traumatic topics have the potential to cause harm" (Nikischer, 2018, p. 906). Indeed, IRBs and similar supervisory organs such as ethical review boards and research ethics boards, have been slow to adopt anything like systemic requirements for assessing researcher well-being as part of the human subjects approval process (Dickson-Swift et al., 2008). Unfortunately, this leaves responsibility for identifying and managing researcher trauma to the individual researcher.

Managing researcher trauma when using social media as social science data therefore requires a researcher to be cognizant of the signs of such trauma both upon herself and her research team. Bride, Radey, and Figley (2007) provides a rundown of specific batteries of psychological self-tests that may be helpful for researchers to implement depending on their particular research team design. The Headington Institute, an American Psychological Association–approved nonprofit dedicated to providing psychological support for workers and researchers at risk for vicarious trauma has a variety of online resources and tests available, in addition to a guide written to summarize warning signs and coping strategies (Pearlman and McKay, 2008).

In addition to these general resources, there are a number of concerns that researchers studying social media in particular should be aware of.

Undergraduate research assistants can be particularly vulnerable to vicarious trauma. They are generally younger with less adult experience in dealing with any form of trauma, vicarious or not. Their position hand coding social media data is most likely to be for pay, and not necessarily because of an interest or passion in the particular subject matter being coded. As a result, traumatic content can blindside them in comparison to a team member who has consciously chosen to study the specific trauma they might be exposed to in the course of this research.

This presents a larger issue when delegating coding to paid assistants recruited externally for that specific task, whether undergraduates or not.

Researchers who have personally experienced trauma are more likely to experience vicarious trauma when exposed to similar trauma in others (Pearlman and McKay, 2008). But without a close personal relationship with assistants, it is difficult for a researcher to monitor and evaluate the emotional well-being of team members, or to know whether certain material represents triggering material for them due to traumatic and private events in their past (Etherington, 2007).

The ease of collecting data from social media means that it is increasingly common for projects to span languages that the primary investigator does not know, with coding of the collected data delegated to paid assistants fluent in the appropriate languages. This is an exciting scientific opportunity in many fields as it can add a generalized and cross-country dimension to research, but it also represents an added level of risk for vicarious trauma. When the supervisory researcher cannot know first-hand the severity of the material to which their researchers are exposed, it is an additional barrier to protecting those researchers from harm.

Similar concerns apply to graduate students, as often they are recruited into projects in order to hand code images and text, while the researcher in charge focuses on aggregated numbers and statistics. While there is nothing inherently wrong with this sort of division of labor, when there is traumatic material involved it can inadvertently turn into a delegation of emotional labor to those not in a position to set limits. Graduate students are faced with extraordinary pressure to prove themselves and finish assigned tasks. They will often be hesitant to express any difficulty for fear of being labeled incompetent or not having what it takes to do this job. Supervisory faculty have a responsibility to their graduate students, whether working independently or on faculty projects, to ensure that research does not traumatize.

One of the great opportunities afforded by social media data is that the low barrier to entry means that original data collection is now possible for both undergraduate and graduate students for their own research projects with essentially no resources. This is a profoundly powerful pedagogical tool, with undergraduates able to collect data from around the world on topics of their own choosing, where a generation before that was locked away behind research grants and graduate school admissions. But this dropping of barriers has a dark side as well: easy access to some of the most traumatic things the world has, potentially exposing students to harm.

For example, in teaching my own undergraduate Internet and Politics courses that require research projects, nearly every semester a student is interested in researching how terrorist groups use social media or a similar such project. These are salient research questions, arrived at in good faith by bright students interested in security topics. But in practical terms, it can mean a 19-year-old seeking out and reading propaganda that has been specifically designed to recruit 19-year-olds into terrorist groups. There are no easy answers to this dilemma. The best a professor can do is be aware of the risks, and be open and transparent with students as to what those risks are, while nudging independent research away from such shoals.

Faculty and research leads are of course not immune to vicarious trauma, and in certain ways are even more at risk. The Sexual Violence Research Initiative has published guidelines on risk factors and warning signs of vicarious trauma (Nikischer, 2018). One of particular concern for faculty is the risk factor of "working in isolation," which is the norm for many academic researchers. The pressure of tenure-track positions can further contribute to such issues, making it difficult for researchers to give themselves the time they need to emotionally cope with exposure to traumatic content. Additional research has shown that in fields where peer support is stronger and more common, vicarious trauma is less of a problem (Manning-Jones, De Terte, and Stephens, 2016).

There are no magic bullets to dealing with the risks of vicarious trauma, other than approaching the problem in a good faith effort to take care of both yourself and your research team. Monitor your students, research assistants, and yourself for emotional and behavioral changes by encouraging transparency and having regular check-ins and meetings.

6.4 A Researcher's Perspective

In 2014, I presented my work publicly at a scholarly conference for one of the first times in my career. The particular work in question was a project using geocoded Twitter data to study how mass protests and violence unfold in real time at a micro-level, focusing in particular on the Euromaidan protests in Ukraine that had happened earlier that year. The project found that it was possible to relatively easily detect the occurrence of mass protest based on nothing but patterns in the way that network-central actors tended to geographically converge during mass events (Wilson, 2017). The utility of the finding was that scholars could detect the occurrence of mass protest even in the absence of free media or reporters on site at the event in question. Figure 6.1 shows one output of that research, a zoomed-in street-level map of central Kiev mapping precisely the origin of tweets and specific instances of violence from the peak days of the revolution.

One audience member took grave offense to the research during the Q&A period, vocally arguing that this sort of research was dangerous, creating new tools for authoritarian regimes to use in monitoring their populations. I present the map in question here because it was the sparking point in this presentation. It

Figure 6.1 Violence (stars) and tweets (dots) in Central Kiev, February 18–20, 2014

was displayed in animated form, with tweets and incidents of violence appearing and fading out as they occurred as 3 days of revolution were compressed into 30 seconds of animation, demonstrating the pattern of how the two were largely independent of each other and constrained to different parts of the map. The audience member was deeply upset because the collected data, if abused, could easily be used by a malicious regime to identify those who were present at the protests. In their mind, there was little distinction between my data collection and dictators compiling lists of protesters. I was lucky enough to have a senior social media scholar serving as moderator on the panel, someone who was accustomed to these arguments and was well equipped to defuse an ugly situation.

Similar objections are often raised when social media data is used in research, asserting that it represents an Orwellian and invasive form of data collection that should raise ethical concerns. There are a number of problems with that interpretation of the collection of social media data. First, it should be noted that social media is inherently *social*. It is data that an individual has intentionally put into the public sphere, and there cannot be a reasonable expectation of privacy when explicitly broadcasting something publicly for others across the Internet to consume. The collection of survey data through knocking on doors, calling personal phones, and asking highly personal questions (which has long been accepted as acceptable in a social scientific context) is vastly more invasive on a personal level than the passive collection of publicly available data.

Additionally, this data is available to anyone with an internet connection and the technical knowledge to download it. One of the foundational motivations of human-subjects ethics in the social sciences is ensuring that those from whom we collect data are not endangered for doing so. Or, to put it more simply, that our research cannot be used by dictators or other power holders to hurt people. But social media data is already public, and the collection of it by academic researchers does not make it more public or usable to those who would abuse it. The resource threshold for collecting such data en masse is so incredibly low, as demonstrated throughout this book, that the idea that social science researchers are collecting data that any malicious actor couldn't already collect themselves if interested is patently absurd. To put it even more strongly: Because this data is readily accessible by those who would abuse it, it is irresponsible for academic researchers to *not* use it.

That is not to say that privacy concerns should be discarded entirely though, as there are very real ethical issues lurking in the gray areas between the straw men of data collection either enabling evil or being a remedy to it. While Twitter data is largely public facing, other social media data isn't, and its users have an expectation of privacy, even if that privacy is routinely broken by the companies that profit off of collecting it in the first place. Take for instance the Cambridge Analytica scandal that was exposed a few months after the 2016 American presidential elections. Using data on nearly 90 million Americans acquired from a third party who had collected the data under the auspices of academic research, Cambridge Analytica ran a massive advertising campaign on social media on behalf of the Trump campaign, using advertising meticulously targeted based on psychological profiles constructed from the data on users. Additional reports revealed similar efforts on behalf of the Leave campaign in the Brexit vote. While the company itself is now subject to criminal investigations (in addition to ceasing to exist), and its actual effect on the elections has been largely deemed a nonfactor, the concern is very real. And, going forward, it is something for scholars to keep in the back of their minds when designing and deploying data collection efforts on social media. Whether users of Facebook were harmed is an argument about the definition of *harm*, because while an election may not have been swung, the users certainly did not consent to their data being used in such a manner. And it is important to note that Facebook's rules did not object to the collection of that data, but only to the way that it was transferred to a for-profit company for independent use. The root of Facebook's objection was twofold: Cambridge Analytica got caught, and someone else was profiting off of the data collected by Facebook.

These issues are intertwined with the principle of informed consent, in that human subjects of research must be able to have an educated opinion on whether they consent to the research in question. On the one hand, social media data that is publicly available should not be reasonably considered private, and that by posting data publicly (and abiding by appropriate terms of use on such sites), individuals are implicitly consenting to the public consumption of that data. On the other hand, it is a stretch to assume that the users of these platforms have consented in a truly *informed* capacity with regard to just how much of their data is recorded and what is available. Consider tweets that have their GPS coordinates attached by the device of the poster. While that user may understand that anyone can read what they tweeted, most of the public has little understanding that if they are using the geocoded-enabled app on their phone, latitude and longitude coordinates precise enough to tell which room of their house they were in when they hit send, are readily available to any programmer with access to the Twitter API, whether they are employed by corporations, governments, or universities.

The examples above tend to deal with large aggregated sets of social media data, which provides a compromise approach in that all academically published data generated as a result of this data collection might be presented in aggregate form, limiting any conceivable harm to individuals whose data has been collected. As an additional gray area though, consider the growing phenomenon of "cyborgs," which are social media accounts that combine automated bot activity and normal human usage. Often, these accounts will be those of "real" people who have provided their login credentials (often for a nominal payment) to a third party in order to post their own automated content. This allows the basic activity of bots to proceed under cover generated by the person's actual social media posting, making them much harder to detect algorithmically. What reasonable expectation of privacy does an individual have who sells control of their account in this way?

There are no good answers and no established sets of rules to the issues raised in this section. Refusing to use publicly available data on ethical grounds of informed consent and privacy seems naive and self-sabotaging when the data exists and is being exploited by private and state actors with impunity. However, researchers do have a moral obligation to consider their data collection through an ethical lens, to consider whether there is conceivable harm to their research subjects when making use of this data. Throughout this book, we have developed a variety of tools for collecting and analyzing data, but it is important to remember that the data in question is the thoughts and words of human beings, and the implications of how and what we are collecting are still being formalized and worked through.

This is the cutting edge, not just of research data, but of our own development as a society. We are only beginning to understand what the effect of social media is on our civilization, and so using the data we can pull from it in order to understand our society and politics better is going to be a moving target of methods, mechanisms, and ethics. Operate in good faith, and try to give back understanding at least in proportion to the footprint you leave.

References

Alkulaib, Lulwah, Abdulaziz Alhamadani, Taoran Ji, and Chang-Tien Lu (2019). "Collect ethically: reduce bias in Twitter datasets." In *Annual International Symposium on Information Management and Big Data*. Springer, pp. 106–114.

Anastasopoulos, L. Jason, Dhruvil Badani, Crystal Lee, Shiry Ginosar, and Jake Williams (2016). "Photographic home styles in Congress: a computer vision approach." *arXiv preprint arXiv:1611.09942.*

Anastasopoulos, L. Jason, Dhruvil Badani, Crystal Lee, Shiry Ginosar, and Jake Ryland Williams (2017). "Political image analysis with deep neural networks." University of Georgia.

Anderson, Benedict (1983). *Imagined Communities: Reflections on the Origin and Spread of Nationalism.* Verso.

Bailey, Michael, David Dittrich, and Erin Kenneally (2013). "Applying ethical principles to information and communication technology research." URL: www.dhs.gov/csd-resources.

Bailey, Michael, David Dittrich, Erin Kenneally, and Doug Maughan (2012). "The Menlo report: ethical principles guiding information and communication technology research." URL: www.dhs.gov/sites/default/files/publications/CSD-MenloPrinciplesCORE-20120803_1.pdf.

Bollen, Johan, Huina Mao, and Xiaojun Zeng (2011). "Twitter mood predicts the stock market." *Journal of Computational Science* 2.1, pp. 1–8.

Bride, Brian E., Melissa Radey, and Charles R. Figley (2007). "Measuring compassion fatigue." *Clinical Social Work Journal* 35.3, pp. 155–163.

Campan, Alina, Tobel Atnafu, Traian Marius Truta, and Joseph Nolan (2018). "Is data collection through Twitter streaming API useful for academic research?" In *2018 IEEE International Conference on Big Data (Big Data)*. IEEE, pp. 3638–3643.

Castells, Manuel (2015). *Networks of Outrage and Hope: Social Movements in the Internet Age.* Polity.

Castillo, Carlos (2016). *Big Crisis Data: Social Media in Disasters and Time-Critical Situations.* Cambridge University Press,

Chadwick, Andrew and Philip N. Howard (2010), *Routledge Handbook of Internet Politics.* Taylor & Francis.

Chen, Kaiping, Zening Duan, and Sijia Yang (2021). "Twitter as research data: tools, costs, skill sets, and lessons learned." *Politics and the Life Sciences* 41.1, pp. 1–17.

Chuang, Jason, Christopher D. Manning, and Jeffrey Heer (2012). "Termite: visualization techniques for assessing textual topic models." In *Proceedings of the International Working Conference on Advanced Visual Interfaces*, pp. 74–77.

Clifton, Chris (2015). "Ethics review process as a foundation for ethical thinking." URL:https://bigdata.fpf.org/wp-content/uploads/2015/12/Clifton-Ethical-Review-Process-as-a-Foundatio-for-Ethical-Thinking.pdf

Colneric, Niko and Janez Demsar (2020). "Emotion recognition on Twitter: comparative study and training a unison model." In *IEEE Transactions on Affective Computing* 11.3, pp. 433–446.

CSMaP (2022). *CSMaP Data Collections and Analysis Tools.* DOI: 10.5281/zenodo.5090728. URL: https://csmapnyu.org/data-collections-and-analysis-tools/.

Data.gov (2020), *Data.gov.* URL: www.data.gov/.

Dickson-Swift, Virginia, Erica L James, Sandra Kippen, and Pranee Liamputtong (2008). "Risk to researchers in qualitative research on sensitive topics: issues and strategies." *Qualitative Health Research* 18.1, pp. 133–144.

Diesner, Jana and Chieh-Li Chin (2015). "Usable ethics: practical considerations for responsibly conducting research with social trace data." *Big Data Ethics.* URL: https://bigdata.fpf.org/papers/usable-ethics-practical-considerations-for-responsibly-conducting-research-with-social-trace-data/.

Dingwall, Robert (2017). "Social sciences lose out again in Common Rule reform." *Nature Human Behaviour* 1.4, p. 1.

Dutton, William H. (2013). *The Oxford Handbook of Internet Studies.* Oxford University Press.

Etherington, Kim (2007). "Working with traumatic stories: from transcriber to witness." *International Journal of Social Research Methodology* 10.2, pp. 85–97.

Farrell, Henry (2012). "The consequences of the internet for polities." *Annual Review of Political Science* 15.1, pp. 35–52.

Figley, Charles R. (1985). *Trauma and its Wake.* Routledge.

Figley, Charles R. (1995). *Compassion Fatigue: Coping with Secondary Traumatic Stress Disorder in Those Who Treat the Traumatized.* Brunner-Routledge.

Figley, Charles R. (2002). *Treating Compassion Fatigue.* Brunner-Routledge.

Figley, Charles R. and Robert G. Roop (2006). *Compassion Fatigue in the Animal Care Community.* Humane Society Press.

Franzke, Aline Shakti, Anja Bechmann, Michael Zimmer, Charles Ess, and the Association of Internet Researchers (2020). *Internet Research: Ethical Guidelines 3.0.* Tech, rep. Association of Internet Researchers.

Fuchs, Christian (2017). *Social Media: A Critical Introduction.* Sage.

GADM (2020). *Database of Global Administrative Areas.* URL: https://gadm.org/.

Gallego, Jorge, Juan David Martinez, Kevin Munger, and Mateo Vásquez-Cortés (Dec. 2019). "Tweeting for peace: experimental evidence from the 2016 Colombian plebiscite." *Electoral Studies* 62, p. 102072.

Garfinkel, Simson (2017). "Beyond IRBs: designing ethical review processes for big data research." *Future of Privacy Forum.* URL: https://fpf.org/2016/01/15/winning-privacy-papers-for-policymakers/.

Gellner, Ernest (Dec. 1983). *Nations and Nationalism*. Cornell University Press.

Gelman, Jeremy and Steven Wilson (2021). "Measuring congressional partisanship and its consequences." *Legislative Studies Quarterly* 47.1, pp. 225–256.

Gelman, Jeremy, Steven Lloyd Wilson, and Constanza Sanhueza Petrarca (2021). "Mixing messages: how candidates vary in their use of Twitter." *Journal of Information Technology & Politics* 18.1, pp. 101–115,

Guess, Andrew, Jonathan Nagler, and Joshua Tucker (2019). "Less than you think: prevalence and predictors of fake news dissemination on Faeebook." *Science Advances* 5.1, eaau4586.

Halavais, Alexander (2011). "Open up online research." *Nature* 480.7376, pp. 174–175.

Hashemi, Layla, Steven Lloyd Wilson, and Constanza Sanhueza Petrarca (2022). "Investigating the Iranian twittersphere: five hundred days of Farsi Twitter: an overview of what Farsi Twitter looks like, what we know about it, and why it matters." *Journal of Quantitative Description: Digital Media* 2, pp. 1–29.

HCIRB/BRP/DCCPS (2019). *Human Subjects Considerations for Social Media Research*. URL: https://cancercontrol.cancer.gov/sites/default/files/2020-06/human-subjects-considerations-for-social-media-research.pdf.

Hibbin, Rebecca A., Gabrielle Samuel, and Gemma E. Derrick (2018). "From 'a fair game' to 'a form of covert research': research ethics committee members' differing notions of consent and potential risk to participants within social media research." *Journal of Empirical Research on Human Research Ethics* 13.2, pp. 149–159.

Hill, Kashmir (2019). "How cartographers for the U.S. military inadvertently created a house of horrors in South Africa." URL: https://gizmodo.com/how-cartographers-for-the-u-s-military-inadvertently-c-1830758394.

Howard, Philip N., Aiden Duffy, Deen Freelon, et al. (2011). "Opening closed regimes: what was the role of social media during the Arab Spring?" Available at SSRN 2595096.

Jansen, Bernard J., Mimi Zhang, Kate Sobel, and Abdur Chowdhury (2009). "Twitter power: tweets as electronic word of mouth." *Journal of the American Society for Information Science and Technology* 60.11, pp. 2169–2188.

Joo, Jungseock and Zachary C. Steinert-Threlkeld (2018). "Image as data: automated visual content analysis for political science." *arXiv preprint arXiv:1810.01544*.

Jost, John T., Pablo Barberá, Richard Bonneau, et al. (Feb. 2018). "How social media facilitates political protest: information, motivation, and social networks." *Political Psychology* 39, pp. 85–118.

Kummu, Matti, Maija Taka, and Joseph H. A. Guillaume (Feb. 2018). "Gridded global datasets for Gross Domestic Product and Human Development Index over 1990–2015." *Scientific Data* 5.1, pp. 1–15.

Lapowsky, Issie (2019). "Your old tweets give away more location data than you think." URL: www.wired.com/story/twitter-location-data-gps-privacy/.

Lazer, David, Eszter Hargittai, Deen Freelon, et al. (2021). "Meaningful measures of human society in the twenty-first century." *Nature* 595.7866, pp. 189–196,

Lerman, Kristina and Rumi Ghosh (2010). "Information contagion: an empirical study of the spread of news on Digg and Twitter social networks." *arXiv preprint arXiv:1003.2664.*

Lewis, Kevin, Jason Kaufman, Marco Gonzalez, Andreas Wimmer, and Nicholas Christakis (2008). "Tastes, ties, and time: a new social network dataset using Facebook.com." *Social Networks* 30, pp. 330–342.

Littman, Justin (2017). *115th U.S. Congress Tweet Ids.* Version V5, DOI: 10.7910/DVN/UIVHQR.

Littman, Justin (2018). *Ireland 8th Tweet Ids.* Version VI. DOI: 10.7910/DVN/PYCLPE.

Loyle, Cyanne E. and Alicia Simoni (2017). Researching under fire: political science and researcher trauma. *PS – Political Science and Politics* 50.1, pp. 141–145.

Manning-Jones, Shekinah, Ian De Terte, and Christine Stephens (2016). "Secondary traumatic stress, vicarious posttraumatic growth, and coping among health professionals: a comparison study." *New Zealand Journal of Psychology* 45.1, pp. 20–29.

Markham, Annette and Elizabeth Buchanan (2012). *Ethical Decision-Making and Internet Research: Version 2.0.* Tech. rep. August. Association of Internet Researchers, pp. 1–17. URL: https://scholar.google.com/scholar?q=aoir+guidelines%7B%5C&%7DbtnG=%7B%5C&%7Dhl=en%7B%5C&%7Das%7B%5C%7Dsdt=0,3%7B%5C#%7D1.

Mechkova, Valeriya, Daniel Pemstein, Brigitte Seim, and Steven Wilson (2019). "Digital Society Project dataset vl." URL: http://digitalsocietyproject.org/data/.

Mechkova, Valeriya and Steven Lloyd Wilson (2021). "Norms and rage: gender and social media in the 2018 U.S. mid-term elections." *Electoral Studies* 69, p. 102268.

Metzger, Megan, Mac Duffee and Joshua A. Tucker (2017). "Social media and Euro-Maidan: a review essay." *Slavic Review* 76.1, pp. 169–191.

Morstatter, Fred, Jürgen Pfeffer, and Huan Liu (2014). "When is it biased? Assessing the representativeness of Twitter's streaming API." In *Proceedings of the 23rd International Conference on World Wide Web*, pp. 555–556.

Munger, Kevin (Sept. 2017). "Tweetment effects on the tweeted: experimentally reducing racist harassment." *Political Behavior* 39.3, pp. 629–649.

Munger, Kevin (June 2021). "Don't @ me: experimentally reducing partisan incivility on Twitter." *Journal of Experimental Political Science* 8.2, pp. 102–116.

Munger, Kevin, Richard Bonneau, Jonathan Nagler, and Joshua A. Tucker (Oct. 2019). "Elites tweet to get feet off the streets: measuring regime social media strategies during protest." *Political Science Research and Methods* 7.4, pp. 815–834.

Munger, Kevin, Patrick J. Egan, Jonathan Nagler, Jonathan Ronen, and Joshua Tucker (Jan. 2022). "Political knowledge and misinformation in the era of social media: evidence from the 2015 UK election." *British Journal of Political Science* 52.1, pp. 107–127.

Naser, Curtis (2015). "The IRB Sledge-Hammer, Freedom and Big Data." *Big Data Ethics*. URL: https://bigdata.fpf.org/papers/the-irb-sledge-hammer-freedom-and-big-data/.

National Commission for the Protection of Human Subjects of Biomedical and Behavioral Research (1978). "Belmont report: ethical principles and guidelines for the protection of human subjects of research, report of the National Commission for the Protection of Human Subjects of Biomedical and Behavioral Research." URL: https://videocast.nih.gov/pdf/ohrp%7B%5C_%7Dbelmont%7B%5C_%7Dreport.pdf.

Nikischer, Andrea (2018). "Vicarious trauma inside the academe: understanding the impact of teaching, researching and writing violence." *Higher Education* 77, pp. 909–916.

Nordhaus, William, Qazi Azam, David Corderi, et al. (2006). *The G-Econ Database on Gridded Output: Methods and Data 1*. Tech. rep. Yale University.

Padmakumar, Vishakh and Zhanna Terechshenko (Dec. 2020). *SMAPPNYU/ SMaBERTa*. DOI: 10.5281/zenodo.5090728.

Pearlman, Laurie Anne and Lisa McKay (2008). "Understanding and addressing vicarious trauma." URL: www.headington-institute.org.

Pearlman, Laurie Anne and Karen W. Saakvitne (1995). *Trauma and the Therapist: Counter-Transference and Vicarious Traumatization in Psychotherapy with Incest Survivors*. W.W. Norton & Co.

Persily, Nathaniel, and Joshua A. Tucker (2020). *Social Media and Democracy: The State of the Field, Prospects for Reform*. SSRC Anxieties of Democracy, Cambridge University Press.

Petrarca, Constanza Sanhueza, Maria Tyrberg, and Steven Lloyd Wilson (2019). "The 2018 Swedish election campaign on Twitter." *Statsvetenskaplig Tidskrift (Swedish Journal of Political Science)* 121.3, pp. 367–392.

Reed, Philip J., Emma S. Spiro, and Carter T. Butts (Sept. 2016). "Thumbs up for privacy?: differences in online self-disclosure behavior across national cultures." *Social Science Research* 59, pp. 155–170.

Romero, Daniel M., Wojciech Galuba, Sitaram Asur, and Bernardo A. Huberman (2011). "Influence and passivity in social media." In *Joint European Conference on Machine Learning and Knowledge Discovery in Databases*. Springer, pp. 18–33.

Rudinac, Stevan, Iva Gornishka, and Marcel Worring (2017). "Multimodal classification of violent online political extremism content with graph convolutional networks." In *Thematic Workshops '17: Proceedings of the Thematic Workshops of ACM Multimedia 2017*, pp. 245–252.

Ruths, Derek and Jürgen Pfeffer (Nov. 2014). "Social media for large studies of behavior." *Science* 346.6213, pp. 1063–1064.

Sanderson, Zeve, Megan A. Brown, Richard Bonneau, Jonathan Nagler, and Joshua A. Tucker (Aug. 2021). "Twitter flagged Donald Trump's tweets with election misinformation: they continued to spread both on and off the platform." *Harvard Kennedy School Misinformation Review* 2.

Secretary's Advisory Committee on Human Research Protections (2013). "Considerations and Recommendations Concerning Internet Research and Human Subjects Research Regulations, with, Revisions." URL: www.wellesley.edu/sites/default/files/assets/departments/sponsres/files/sachrp%7B%5C_%7Dguidelines%7B%5C_%7Don%7B%5C_%7Dinternet%7B%5C_%7Dresearch%7B%5C_%7D2013.pdf.

SEDAC (2020). *Socioeconomic Data and Applications Center / SEDAC*. URL: https://sedac.ciesin.columbia.edu/.

Shirky, Clay (Feb. 2009). *Here Comes Everybody: The Power of Organizing Without Organizations*. Reprint. Penguin Non-Classics.

Si, Jianfeng, Arjun Mukherjee, Bing Liu, et al. (2013). "Exploiting topic based Twitter sentiment for stock prediction." In *Proceedings of the 51st Annual Meeting of the Association for Computational Linguistics (Volume 2: Short Papers)*, pp. 24–29.

Sievert, Carson and Kenneth Shirley (2014). "LDAvis: a method for visualizing and interpreting topics." In *Proceedings of the Workshop on Interactive Language Learning, Visualization, and Interfaces*, pp. 63–70.

Starbird, Kate (July 2019). "Disinformation's spread: bots, trolls and all of us." *Nature* 571.7766, pp. 449-450.

Steinert-Threlkeld, Zachary C. (Jan. 2018). *Twitter as Data*. Cambridge University Press.

Tene, Omer and Jules Polonetsky (2015). "Beyond IRBs: ethical guidelines for data research," Washington & Lee Law Review Online 72.3.

Tilly, Charles (2002). *Stories, Identities, and Political Change*. Rowman & Littlefield.

Tilly, Charles (2003). *The Politics of Collective Violence*. Cambridge University Press.

Torres, Michelle and Francisco Cantú (2022). "Learning to see: convolutional neural networks for the analysis of social science data." *Political Analysis* 30.1, pp. 113–131.

Tucker, Joshua A., Andrew Guess, Pablo Barberá, et al. (Mar. 2018). "Social media, political polarization, and political disinformation: a review of the scientific literature." *SSRN Electronic Journal*. DOI: 10.2139/SSRN.

Tufekci, Zeynep and Christopher Wilson (2012). "Social media and the decision to participate in political protest: observations from Tahrir Square." *Journal of Communication* 62.2, pp. 363–379.

Twitter (2018). "Developer agreement and policy – Twitter developers (effective: May 25, 2018)." URL: https://developer.twitter.com/en/developer-terms/agreement-and-policy.

Twitter (2019), "Twitter support on Twitter: 'Most people don't tag their precise location in Tweets, so we're removing this ability to simplify your Tweeting experience. You'll still be able to tag your precise location in Tweets through our updated camera. It's helpful.'" URL: https://twitter.com/TwitterSupport/status/1141039841993355264.

Vaccari, Cristian (2013). *Digital Politics in Western Democracies: A Comparative Study*. JHU Press.

Vayena, Effy. Urs Gasser, Alexandra Wood, David O'Brien, and Micha Altman (2016). "Elements of a new ethical framework for big data research." *Washington and Lee Law Review Online* 72(3): Article 5.

Vayena, Effy and John Tasioulas (2016). "The dynamics of big data and human rights: the ease of scientific research." *Philosophical Transactions of the Royal Society A: Mathematical, Physical and Engineering Sciences* 374.2083.

Vieweg, Sarah, Amanda C. Hughes, Kate Starbird, and Leysia Palen (2010). "Microblogging during two natural hazards events: what Twitter may contribute to situational awareness." In: *Proceedings of the SIGCHI Conference on Human Factors in Computing Systems*, pp. 1079–1088.

Wilson, Steven Lloyd (2016). "Information and revolution." PhD thesis. University of Wisconsin, Madison.

Wilson, Steven Lloyd (2017). "Detecting mass protest through social media." *Journal of Social Media in Society* 6.2, pp. 5–25.

Wilson, Steven Lloyd, Staffan Lindberg, and Kjetil Tronvoll (2021). "The best and worst of times: the paradox of social media and Ethiopian polities." *First Monday* 26.10.

Wilson, Steven Lloyd and Charles Wiysonge (2020). "Social media and vaccine hesitancy." *BMJ Global Health* 5.10, e004206.

Wilson, Tom and Kate Starbird (Jan. 2020). "Cross-platform disinformation campaigns: lessons learned and next steps." *Harvard Kennedy School Misinformation Review* 1.1.

Won, Donghyeon, Zachary C. Steinert-Threlkeld, and Jungseock Joo (2017). "Protest activity detection and perceived violence estimation from social media images." In *Proceedings of the 25th ACM International Conference on Multimedia*, pp. 786–794.

Woodby, Lesa L., Beverly Williams, Angelina R. Wittich, and Kathryn L. Burgio (2011). Expanding the notion of researcher distress: the cumulative effects of coding. *Qualitative Health Research* 21.6, pp. 830–838.

Xi, Nan, Di Ma, Marcus Liou, et al. (2020). "Understanding the political ideology of legislators from social media images." In *Proceedings of the International AAAI Conference on Web and Social Media*. Vol. 14, pp. 726–737.

Ying, Qing, Matthew C. Hansen, Peter V. Potapov, et al. (June 2017). "Global bare ground gain from 2000 to 2012 using Landsat imagery." *Remote Sensing of Environment* 194, pp. 161–176.

Yang, Kai-Cheng, Onur Varol, Clayton A. Davis, et al. (Jan. 2019). "Arming the public with artificial intelligence to counter social bots." *Human Behavior and Emerging Technologies* 1.1, pp. 48–61.

Zhao, Dejin and Mary Beth Rosson (2009). "How and why people Twitter: the role that micro-blogging plays in informal communication at work." In *Proceedings of the ACM 2009 International Conference on Supporting Group Work*, pp. 243–252.

Zimmer, Michael (2010). "'But the data is already public': on the ethics of research in Faeebook." In: *Ethics and Information Technology* 12.4, pp. 313–325.

Index

CPSIA information can be obtained
at www.ICGtesting.com
Printed in the USA
LVHW082106051222
734570LV00005B/467